THE OPEN ROAD WITHIN

What Motorcycle Touring Teaches You
About Freedom, Happiness and Life –
Whether You Ride Or Not

by
Wayne McDonald

The Open Road Within

First published in 2025

Copyright © Wayne McDonald 2025

All rights reserved. No part of this book may be reproduced or transmitted in any form or by any means, electronic or mechanical, including photocopying, recording or by any information storage and retrieval system, without permission in writing from the publisher. The *Australian Copyright Act* (the Act) allows a maximum of one chapter or 10 per cent of this book, whichever is greater, to be photocopied by any educational institution for its educational purposes, provided that the educational institution (or body that administers it) has given a remuneration notice to the Copyright Agency (Australia) under the Act.

Wayne McDonald asserts his right to be known as the author of this work.

Published by Wayne McDonald
Adelaide, South Australia
www.successknowhow.com.au

Wayne McDonald acknowledges the Traditional Owners of the Country on which he lives and works. He pays his respects to Aboriginal and Torres Strait Islander Elders, past and present.

A catalogue record for this book is available from the National Library of Australia.

ISBN: 978-1-7643412-0-2

Dedication

*For my children, Oliver, Georgia and Archie,
and for my loving wife, Miranda,
who has supported my obsession
with motorcycles from day one.*

The Open Road Within

CONTENTS

Introduction 6

Chapter 1
Only a Biker Knows Why a Dog Sticks Its Head Out the Car Window 8

Chapter 2:
Planning, Anxiety and the Chatter in Our Head 28

Chapter 3
Decisions, Detours and Risks 54

Chapter 4:
Mindfulness and Emotional Intelligence 72

Chapter 5:
The Psychology of Flow: When Rider and Machine Become One 92

Chapter 6:
Responsibility 107

Chapter 7:
Resilience and Resourcefulness 129

Chapter 8:
Courage, Risk and Commitment 148

Chapter 9
Purpose, Passion and the Power of Clear Direction 169

Chapter 10
The Art of the Long Ride: Endurance and Patience 187

Chapter 11
Riding the Invisible Road: Intuition, Synchronicity and Trust 206

Chapter 12
The Final Ride: Endings, Identity and What Comes After 216

Epilogue - The Road Still Calls 232

INTRODUCTION

There's a joy so strong it cannot be explained. It can only be felt. It lives in the low hum of the engine, the cool sting of morning air, and the gentle blur of the world as you lean into a curve. It's the same instinct that draws a dog to an open car window: a longing to be a part of the world as it rushes past. Dogs aside, only bikers truly understand that feeling. The quiet exhilaration of surrendering to the moment, of becoming one with the road rather than just travelling along it. There's something primal in that pull, something no meeting, schedule or tidy life plan can replicate.

This book is about that pull. The deep, wordless freedom found not just in the open road but also in the open self. The journey may begin with two wheels, but ultimately, it leads inwards.

There's something magical about the open road that calls to us, no matter where we come from. For some, it's the thrill of the unknown. For others, it's the release that comes from leaving behind the noise and routine. For me, as a touring motorcyclist for over fifty years, it's been all that and more.

Motorcycling has been more than a passion. It's been my teacher, my mirror and, sometimes, my confessor. Virtually every kilometre has revealed something – about freedom, happiness and life, and the subtle art of navigating its inevitable twists and turns. Through winding mountain passes, outback straights and coastal curves, I've come to realise that the most important journey isn't the one on the map. It's the one unfolding within.

The road is more than just pavement. It's an unfolding metaphor of the human condition. It humbles you. It teaches you to let go of the illusion of total control, to face fear head on, and to find peace in the unknown. It reminds you that fulfilment isn't about arrival; it's about learning to travel well.

And, like life, the road is both finite and infinite. Any given ride has an endpoint, but the inner journey has no limit. As you change, so does the meaning of the road beneath you. What once felt ordinary becomes sacred. What once felt like just another bend becomes a moment of revelation.

This book invites you to take that deeper journey, with or without a motorcycle. Whether or not you ride, chances are you've felt the pull to break free. To live more fully. To reconnect with your own truth.

That's what The Open Road is about: the ride we can all take if we choose to move through life with greater courage, clarity and heart.

Each chapter explores a key theme such as resilience, mindfulness, flow, commitment and purpose. Each is rooted not just in philosophy and neuroscience but also in lived experience. I've spent over forty years in the personal development field, helping thousands of people navigate change, challenge and transformation. What I've learned is that, in their own way, everyone's a rider on their personal inner journey.

These are not abstract ideas. They're real lessons forged through experience on the road, in the coaching room, and in life's raw, unpredictable moments. The bike just makes them clearer.

This is not a book for motorcyclists. It's a book from one. A guide for anyone ready to live more consciously, love more deeply, and lean into life's curves with eyes open and spirit engaged. Whether that means leaving a job, speaking a long-held truth, or simply learning to enjoy the moment you're in, this book is for you.

So, grab your helmet (metaphorical or otherwise) and join me. The road is waiting. Let's ride!

Chapter 1

ONLY A BIKER KNOWS WHY A DOG STICKS ITS HEAD OUT THE CAR WINDOW

Every morning when we come into the kitchen to get ready for work, Murphy, our three-year-old Cavoodle, waits by the cupboard for his treat. The second it opens, he bounces in circles, anticipation buzzing through his body. His excitement jumps to a whole new level when we grab his leash or open the car door. As soon as he's in the back seat, he's practically vibrating, waiting for that magic moment when the window rolls down, the breeze hits his face, and his nose twitches as it savours the scents of the world. Tongue out, ears flapping, eyes wide open. He's completely alive.

In those moments, it's as if nothing else matters. No worries. No distractions. Just pure, unfiltered joy. Murphy is fully present. No ego, no thought, no identity, no self-doubt. Isn't that the state that mystics and meditators spend their lifetimes seeking? Just pure being, pure joy. Maybe our dogs are onto something. If Murphy could talk, I'm sure he'd be shouting, "This is the best day of my life!"

After watching him, I have realised that that kind of raw, uninhibited joy isn't just for dogs. I know that feeling, too. I feel it every time I ride a motorcycle.

You're flying down the highway. No roof. No walls. No sense of being trapped in a cage. Just you, the wind, and the hum of the engine beneath you. Every sense is alive. Every second is real. There's no pause button. Just the next corner. And the one after that.

Only a Biker Knows Why a Dog Sticks Its Head Out the Car Window

That's why dogs stick their heads out of car windows, and why bikers chase the horizon. It's not just about speed. It's also about presence. Freedom. Aliveness.

Even after decades of travelling on two wheels, each new ride brings with it the same anticipation: the wind on my face; the smells of the world; the sense of freedom known only by motorcyclists (and dogs who ride with their heads sticking out car windows). It's not just the destination that matters; it's also every twist and turn along the way.

This book isn't just about motorcycles. It's about that feeling and so much more. It's about the lessons the road teaches us: how to be free; how to live in the moment; how to face risk and uncertainty with courage; and how to find meaning in every twist and turn. Motorcycling is the perfect metaphor for life because, just like the open road, it's full of surprises, challenges and moments that take your breath away. Over the years, I have come to understand that motorcycling is my teacher. Every stretch of road, every curve, every unexpected detour has carried lessons that go far beyond motorcycling.

On a motorcycle, you can't hide from the realities of the ride. You can feel every bump, every gust of wind, every change in the weather. You're not shielded by a steel cage, as you are in a car, nor can you be distracted by a screen or a book. You're out there, fully exposed, fully alive.

I invite you to join me on this journey – both on the road and within. Let's explore what it means to live fully, to embrace the unknown, and to discover the deep joy that comes from riding the open road within.

This is why we ride. Not because it's safe, but because it's real. And that's what this book is about: finding the real in a world that too often settles for comfort and conformity. It's about facing risk, being present and choosing to live more fully, no matter what twists and turns life presents to you.

For those who don't ride, all is not lost; maybe you've felt it in other ways. At a lookout at sunrise with the wind in your face. Skiing down a mountain. Sailing across a bay. Hiking a remote trail. Driving with the windows down and music up on a perfect day. The activity isn't the important thing; the aliveness and passion for life that it brings is what counts. Whether it's riding, surfing, rock climbing, running, or playing ukulele, many of us are drawn to pursuits that don't necessarily make sense to other people. Motorcycling just happens to be, in my non-biased opinion, the best activity that it is possible to pursue!

Why we ride: The beautiful paradox of motorcycling

My best friend Ian lives on the New South Wales south coast, about four hours south of Sydney. I live in the Adelaide Hills in South Australia. For decades, we have gone motorcycle touring together. And when we have, we've often met up at Halls Gap in Victoria.

Why Halls Gap? Because it has a great Indian restaurant.

Are we mad?

Ian rides 1,059 kilometres over two days to get there. At a mere 487 kilometres, it's just around the corner for me, an easy day's ride. Of course, there are more convenient places to meet. And it's not really about the food at that restaurant. It's about the ride.

To many outsiders, motorcycling is illogical, and motorcyclists are insane. It's an impractical, inefficient, dangerous and often uncomfortable way to travel. You also need to dress like a cross between an astronaut and a gladiator. Cars are safer, warmer and more convenient, and you can hop into a car in shorts and a T-shirt if you want to. You're safely secured in a steel cage with airbags, entertainment and air conditioning – five-star comfort, comparatively. Planes get you there faster. Trains allow you to relax while you travel vast distances. And yet, we ride. Not because it makes sense, but because it's a passion and it simply feels right.

This is the paradox of motorcycling: in a world obsessed with making things safer and easier, we riders deliberately choose the harder path, the path less travelled. We embrace the raw, the inconvenient, the risky and the unpredictable. As Robert M. Pirsig wrote in *Zen and the Art of Motorcycle Maintenance:*

> You see things vacationing on a motorcycle in a way that is completely different from any other. In a car you're always in a compartment, and because you're used to it, you don't realise that through that car window everything you see is just more TV. You're a passive observer and it is all moving by you boringly in a frame.

On a motorcycle, there's no safety net, no filter, just you and the road. You feel the heat and the rain, and you smell the smells. You're not a passenger; you're a part of the scene. That kind of immersion isn't just for riders. As suggested above, you can also find it walking silently in nature, painting without a clock, and dancing until you're breathless. Whatever the activity, it requires you to be fully present – in the moment. And we all need a sense of freedom. Some people think it's about the destination. For us motorcyclists, though, the ride is the destination. It's our way of experiencing a deep sense of aliveness, or as the mythologist Joseph Campbell put it, it's how we "follow our bliss".

One of the most enjoyable and memorable rides I have ever been on took me through northern NSW and through the middle of a storm so violent that it added a day to my trip. The struggle against the elements – the rain, wind, and even hail at one stage – made it into an adventure. Adventure requires courage, risk-taking and resourcefulness. That's what that ride took, and many others like it. Although the conditions were miserable, I loved riding through the storm. And – maybe I am mad! – I grew as a person that day.

The call of the open road

Ian and I have been riding buddies for fifty years. On a recent trip, we rode up to Longreach in northwestern Queensland, then across to Yeppoon on the coast. We covered close to 7,000 kilometres in twenty-six days. As usual, after about a week back at home, we were both itching for another long ride.

People who don't love riding (or driving, for that matter) simply don't get it. Why would anyone waste all that time when you can fly to anywhere in Australia in a few hours? And on a motorbike? I can hear them say, "You must be crazy!" or "You must have a death wish!"

No, not crazy. Just passionate about experiencing the freedom that comes with being on the open road.

"They" say that flying is more efficient. It gets you there in mere hours, and then you can start enjoying yourself. But efficiency depends on one's perspective. In my experience, if it's measured in terms of fun per minute, motorcycling is very efficient. "They" think that the destination is more important than the journey. However, the moment I leave my driveway, I'm having fun. Part of the fun of riding comes from the autonomy and sense of freedom it offers. Many (most?) people want autonomy and freedom, but they are stuck in the grind of their everyday lives. Touring, or even going for a day's ride, gives a welcome break from that sense of captivity to the mundane of life.

Motorcycling – and for me, this is especially true of touring – provides the sense of autonomy and freedom that we all crave. It allows me the freedom to go where I want, when I want, and with whom I want. (You'll see in the following chapter that I am a big advocate for planning, so it is an *organised freedom* – another motorcycling paradox.) There's nothing quite like feeling the wind in your face and noticing slight changes in temperature as you ride an open road that stretches for kilometres in front of you.

Long-distance riding is a metaphor for life. It takes resilience, perseverance, courage and personal responsibility. And self-reliance. Many times, Ian and I find ourselves riding in the middle of nowhere, with poor reception (and in the early days, no phones) – places where, if something happens to us, we're on our own. This is why we travel with a tool kit and a first aid kit. We get ourselves out of trouble most of the time, but we also carry a personal locator beacon so that if all else fails, we can call the cavalry. Thankfully, we have never needed to use it.

Every part of life comes with a myriad of risks, challenges and obstacles. Just like on the open road. The weather, accidents, roadworks, terrible accommodation, animals. And let's not forget incompetent or distracted drivers. Facing these things requires focus, planning, good decision-making, riding skill, judgement and patience. And a host of other attributes.

Motorcycling reflects the reality of life

Not everyone wants to ride. Many people never will, and that's fine. This book isn't a sales pitch for motorcycles. It's all about what riding them reveals, the deeper human truths that are reflected. Riding can even be used as a framework for self-inquiry or self-discovery. One's desires for freedom and purpose or to push through challenges and feel fully alive can be satisfied by activities other than riding on two wheels. But that's what does it for us riders. I believe anyone's life can be enriched by their pursuing a passion and aiming for mastery in it – whatever the passion.

Most of us want to live a full and happy life – to return to what many would say is our natural state of joy and peace. Many yearn for freedom and autonomy. But we all face a myriad of internal and external obstacles and challenges in the way of achieving these things. In Australia and New Zealand, we're fortunate that most of us have some degree of freedom and autonomy in our everyday lives. (Having lived in New Zealand for ten years, and being married to a proud Kiwi, I've experienced both countries firsthand.) Facing challenges and overcoming obstacles is, perhaps, the best personal development course there is.

True freedom comes from having control over our choices, our time, and our direction in life. It means pursuing passions without having to succumb to external pressure, maintaining strong physical and mental well-being, setting firm personal boundaries, and embracing opportunities to explore new places. Living in alignment with our values and principles, breaking routines, and seeking adventure also contribute to this sense of freedom. For motorcyclists, the open road embodies freedom perfectly. It offers movement, presence, and the pure exhilaration of unrestricted exploration. Freedom is not only about outer autonomy but also the inner liberation from fear, conditioning and unconscious reaction. It's choosing how you respond to life – not just where you go.

What is a happy life?

Happiness is a broad, deeply personal and elusive concept that has been defined in many ways throughout history. If freedom and autonomy set the foundation for a fulfilling life, then happiness is the experience of living that life well. Philosophers, psychologists and spiritual traditions have grappled with defining happiness for centuries. Is happiness an enduring state of bliss? A life free from struggle? Or is it something more nuanced, something that isn't given but cultivated?

In today's world, happiness is often marketed as a product; an artificial state achieved through consumption, achievement or external validation. *Buy this, achieve that, buy enough "stuff" and you'll be happy.* But this illusion fades quickly. If this is your definition of happiness, you're probably stressed, bored and burned out. True happiness, as many ancient and modern thinkers have suggested, is not a static destination but a way of being. It's finding inner peace and true self-esteem that doesn't depend on external factors. It emerges not from fleeting pleasures but from how we engage with life itself.

Aristotle called it *eudaimonia*, a life of virtue and purpose. He argued that happiness is not about collecting the right set of circumstances but about striving for excellence in character and action. Living well means pursuing personal growth, building meaningful relationships and contributing to something greater than ourselves. Friendship, good health and even financial stability can enhance happiness, but they alone are not enough.

Centuries later, the Stoic philosopher Epictetus echoed a similar sentiment: "There is only one way to happiness, and that is to cease worrying about things which are beyond the power of our will." A former slave, Epictetus understood firsthand that happiness was not dictated by external conditions but, rather, by one's response to them. His fellow Stoic Seneca viewed happiness as living in harmony with nature and reason, accepting what we cannot change, and focusing on what we can.

The major religions have defined happiness in different ways. The Buddhist perspective offers a simplified definition: There is no path to happiness; happiness is the path. In other words, why wait to feel happy? Happiness is not some future thing to be chased; it exists in the present in the way we engage with each moment. Mindfulness, gratitude and a deep connection to life as it unfolds bring far greater happiness than any distant goal ever could.

Modern psychology builds on these ancient ideas. Brené Brown (researcher, storyteller, and presenter of one of the most popular TED Talks of all time) argues that happiness is built on courage, vulnerability and connection. In her work on vulnerability and wholehearted living, she argues that happiness is closely tied to courage and connection. True happiness, Brown suggests, comes from embracing imperfection, risking emotional exposure, and cultivating gratitude. Positive psychology pioneer Martin Seligman highlights meaning, flow and relationships as the core of a life well lived.

Alexander Lowen, the founder of Bioenergetic Analysis, a body-centred therapy, made a crucial distinction between pleasure and joy. Pleasure, he argued, is a fleeting sensation often tied to physical gratification such as good food, a warm bath or the rush of acceleration on a bike. It is temporary, dissipating as quickly as it arrives. Joy, on the other hand, is a deeper, more sustainable state arising from an authentic connection to oneself and the world. It is the sense of being alive, fully immersed in the moment, free from the constraints of ego and fear.

For me, happiness isn't a finish line to be crossed; it's the journey itself. It's found in the freedom of the open road, the challenges of pushing beyond comfort zones, and the quiet moments of connection and reflection. It's the deep sense of fulfilment that comes from embracing each twist and turn, being fully present, and learning from both the struggles and the open road ahead.

Happiness isn't about collecting more "stuff", nor is it about comfort or ease. It's not the absence of difficulty. Rather, it's the result of turning inwards, travelling the open road within, and living in integrity with your values. When you align with your true self, you find joy in the journey, an enduring happiness that grows from personal growth, meaning and fulfilment in everyday life.

Happiness is about joy rather than fleeting pleasure, presence rather than dwelling on the past or grasping for the future. Responding with courage instead of seeking to control every outcome.

For me, the motorcycle is more than a machine; it's a vehicle for the pursuit of happiness.

Exactly what is the open road within?

The "open road within" is the path to deep joy and happiness. It is a metaphorical journey that each of us can take through the inner landscapes of thought, emotion, courage and character. It speaks to the path beyond the physical, of travelling the open stretch of inner terrain that we navigate as we grow, reflect and confront life's deeper questions. Just as motorcyclists lean into curves, adapt to changing conditions and find freedom in motion, so, too, can we all learn to face our fears, embrace uncertainty and discover who we truly are.

The open road within is a state of being – a mindset of openness, curiosity and conscious living. Ask yourself what drives you, what holds you back, what requires more courage to change, and what lies ahead when you ride with intention. On the open road within, the destination isn't somewhere "out there"; it's a deeper connection to yourself. If you are reading this book, you are on that road.

It is not just about emotion and psychology. It's the spiritual journey, too.

The soul's ride through the terrain of being and possibility. Just as we navigate on physical roads, we also navigate purpose, presence, fear and love. The very act of riding a bike, which requires balance, flow, attention and surrender, is a metaphor for consciousness.

The joy of motorcycling

I sat on a grassy mound near our rented cottage in Harrietville, Victoria, watching the dark storm clouds roll in. The wind picked up, the temperature dropped, and the scent of the forest – earthy, rich, alive – deepened in my nostrils. For a few magic minutes, I was fully present and immersed in the moment.

It struck me how often I feel this way when I ride: completely alive, grateful for the experience, present and in the moment, and joyful in doing something I love. Motorcycling has a way of amplifying life and making me appreciate the simple yet profound joy of existence.

On a motorcycle, joy is found not only in the thrill of speed but also in the rhythm of the ride, the harmony of body and machine connecting with nature as you ride through a forest, and the awareness of the present moment. A perfect corner taken with precision, the golden light of sunrise breaking over a mountain pass, the camaraderie of fellow riders at the end of a long day. These moments carry joy, not just pleasure.

Riding a motorbike gives me a profound sense of freedom and autonomy. It's impossible to be mindless while riding, because every moment requires presence, focus and awareness. More frequently than when I'm anywhere else, when I'm on my bike, I'm in the zone, fully alive and completely in the moment. It's exhilarating! My inner child gets to come out and play, relishing the thrill, the risk, the freedom, and the wind rushing against my face. I don't know if everyone has their version of motorcycling – an outlet, a passion, something that challenges them and fuels their growth. I suspect not everybody does, but I'm certain they all need one. However, you define happiness, one thing is clear: riding motorcycles makes me happy.

Is riding a motorcycle good for your mental health?

It's not just me. There is plenty of anecdotal evidence, and it's now backed by scientific research. Research that highlights the profound impact motorcycling has on mental and emotional well-being. Studies have found that riding reduces stress, enhances cognitive function, builds emotional resilience and fosters a sense of freedom and community.

A study led by neuroscientist Dr. Don Vaughn at UCLA's Semel Institute for Neuroscience and Human Behaviour found that riding for twenty minutes increased heart rate by 11 percent and boosted adrenaline levels by 27 percent – effects comparable to those of light exercise. It also reduced cortisol levels by 28 percent, which is significant, since high cortisol is linked to anxiety, depression and immune system suppression. Additionally, the study showed that motorcycling enhanced sensory focus and increased alertness, much like the effects of caffeine.

Beyond stress relief, motorcycling also sharpens the mind. Research suggests that riding enhances cognitive abilities such as spatial awareness, working memory and reaction times. The process of navigating roads, making split-second decisions and processing varied sensory input keeps the brain active and engaged. The life lesson here is that growth often comes from challenge. Just as riding strengthens cognitive skills, embracing new experiences and pushing through difficulties sharpens the mind and fosters adaptability in all areas of life.

For many riders, including Ian and me, motorcycling acts as a form of therapy, a way to escape daily pressures and regain emotional balance. The rhythm of the ride, the sensation of movement, and the need to be fully present create a profound sense of relief and renewal. This highlights an important truth: healing is sometimes found in movement, not stillness. Whether it's riding, painting, hiking, or another passion, engaging in an activity that you enjoy allows you to disconnect from stress and find flow. It can be a powerful way to restore emotional well-being. One way of looking at emotion is to see it as energy in motion. That movement – whether physical or spiritual – shifts "stuck-ness", unblocks emotion, and awakens parts of us long dormant. Perhaps the bike doesn't just carry us; perhaps it liberates us.

Another key aspect of motorcycling is the unparalleled sense of freedom it provides. The open road, the wind on your skin, and the ability to travel without confinement create a feeling of liberation, which is particularly beneficial for those who are experiencing stress, burnout or emotional stagnation. True freedom, however, starts with mindset. The open road serves as a reminder that breaking free from limitations, whether physical, emotional or mental, requires a willingness to ride the open road within and embrace adventure, take risks and step outside of comfort zones. And while riding a motorcycle is one way that points the way to the road within, it's not the only way. Find your version of the open road, whatever it is that breaks the routine, awakens your senses and brings you back to yourself.

The hand wave connection

It's an unspoken rule of the open road. A silent bond among riders. When another motorcyclist passes in the opposite direction, you wave. Especially on country roads. Why? Because you're part of a tribe.

Humans seek out connection and purpose. Being part of a tribe gives us a sense of belonging, a shared identity that reinforces our values and aspirations. As a motorcyclist, you are part of something bigger – a brotherhood, a sisterhood, a community bound by the love of the ride. Riders get it. They understand why they're out there in the rain, pushing through the wind, embracing the elements. They recognise the effort, the skill, the passion.

And they know you do, too. That simple wave says it all.

Other experiences of the biker tribe

I now prefer solo or small-group rides, but I've ridden with groups like the Ulysses Club for years. Motorcycling fosters deep bonds through riding together, sharing stories, and creating connections. Harvard's 85-year-long

Study of Adult Development found that strong relationships are the most significant factor in long-term happiness. This underscores the principle that life's journey is richer when shared. Whether through motorcycling or any other shared passion, meaningful connections enhance our experience and remind us that we're never truly alone.

So, is motorcycling good for emotional and mental health? The evidence strongly suggests it is. As already indicated, that certainly is the case for Ian and me. My wife Miranda knows it, too. Although I don't experience anxiety or low moods very often, when I do, Miranda usually asks me, "How long since you've been for a ride?" If it's been more than a few days, she does what she can to support me to get out on the bike. While it's not a substitute for professional mental health treatment, it can be a valuable tool for managing stress, improving cognitive function and fostering emotional resilience. The road ahead isn't just about the destination; it's also a lot to do with the clarity, freedom and connection we find along the way.

Happiness and growth occur through difficulty

Over the past couple of decades, stress and anxiety levels have risen significantly across many countries. Australia has experienced a sharp increase in mental health challenges across various demographics. In both the UK and the US, studies show that rates of anxiety, depression and stress among adolescents and young adults (ages 16–24) have more than doubled. Social psychologist Jonathan Haidt explores this troubling trend in his book The *Anxious Generation*.

According to the Australian Bureau of Statistics' National Study of Mental Health and Wellbeing 2020-21, more than two out of five Australians aged 16 to 85 have experienced a mental disorder at some point in their lives. One in five has had a mental health condition within the past year, anxiety being the most common. The Australian Institute of Health and Welfare reports that the average mental health score for Australians aged 15 to 34 declined from 72 in 2001 to 65 in 2021, reflecting a worsening trend in the younger generations.

Life has always been challenging, but modern Western culture increasingly emphasises minimising discomfort, reducing risk, and prioritising safety. Programs like "Are You OK?" encourage conversations around mental health, but the topic remains difficult for many. Meanwhile, the constant drumbeat of tragedy and disaster on the nightly news reinforces the perception that the world is a dangerous and scary place, fostering a mindset of excessive caution. Have we, in our relentless pursuit of safety, inadvertently contributed to rising anxiety and stress?

Today's technology shields us from discomfort. Our cars have climate control, safety cages, ergonomic seats, lane assist, parking assist and cruise control. Travel is optimised for efficiency, minimising effort and maximising comfort and security.

Motorcyclists, however, embrace the opposite. On every ride, we invite complexity and risk. We experience discomfort as we take the long way home, because it's a better ride. We pack light because we must. We check the weather, because it matters. We accept the rain, wind and heat not as inconveniences but as part of the experience.

Perhaps, in stepping beyond comfort and control, we rediscover something essential: resilience, adaptability and the joy of embracing life as it comes. Henry Cole, a well-known lifelong English motorcyclist, author and documentary presenter, puts it best in his book *A Biker's Tale:* "It's not about speed or bravado. It's about the visceral joy of riding when it's just you, the machine, and the road."

There is joy in doing rather than watching. In being fully part of the journey; not simply a passenger on the ride but engaging fully. In a world that too often encourages efficiency, detachment and getting to the next thing in life as quickly as possible, we embrace the challenge of mastering the moment. And if you're not a motorcyclist, that's okay. You don't need an engine beneath you to chase that feeling. The deeper point is this: Joy often lives on the other side of effort. It's there in the doing, the striving, and the engagement with what you're doing. Whether you find that in a marathon, a gardening project, sailing on a rough sea or building something from scratch, the committed engagement, not the activity, is what matters.

Breaking Free from Anxiety: A Stoic Approach

The Stoics didn't use the modern term "anxiety", but they discussed concepts related to it. They believed in the importance of mastering one's emotions and cultivating calmness and tranquillity, often using terms such as "disturbance" or "unease" to describe the kind of inner turmoil we might now associate with anxiety.

For the Stoics, the root of such emotions, including anxiety, was the attachment to things outside one's control. They taught that we should focus only on what is within our power, for example, our thoughts, actions and responses, while accepting that external events are beyond our control. (I deal with this in detail later in the book.) This idea is central to their philosophy and is exemplified in the teachings of Epictetus and Marcus Aurelius, the Stoic Emperor.

Epictetus explained this idea well when he said, "It's not things themselves that disturb us, but our opinions about them." He believed that what leads to emotional unrest, including anxiety, is the way we interpret external events. If we view them as harmful or threatening, we react with distress. But if we change our interpretation and realise that we cannot control the events, only our reactions to them, we can find peace.

Marcus Aurelius repeatedly reflected on how to maintain equanimity in the face of external stressors such as duties, challenges and even human shortcomings. He writes, "You have power over your mind, not outside events. Realise this, and you will find strength." This teaches us that by shifting our mindset, we can diminish the impact of external stressors on our emotional well-being.

A motorcycling moment: Conquering fear with focus

There was a time when I was heading down an unfamiliar mountain road in Queensland's hinterland, the kind of low-speed, winding, steep stretch that can intimidate even the most seasoned rider. It was a beautiful day, but I found myself gripped by anxiety. The tight bends and the thought of losing control had my mind racing. My heart rate was elevated, and I felt tension in my shoulders, the kind that you know isn't just physical.

As I approached each curve, my body tensed up, but I knew from years of riding that this was a pattern; I had had this mind-based response before. Just as the Stoics taught, I knew I couldn't control the road or the curves, but I could control my reactions. I focused on breathing in deeply and steadily and breathing out slowly and deliberately, just as I would if I were meditating.

Then, in the midst of the ride, I remembered a key Stoic principle: *You have power over your mind, not outside events.* The road, the weather, the tight curves – none of those things were within my control. But how I responded, how I handled the fear, was entirely mine. I shifted my mindset, focusing not on the fear of the bend but on my ability to navigate it with mindfulness. Slowly, the anxiety began to melt away, and I found a rhythm in the flow between rider and machine.

By the time I reached the bottom of the hill, I had moved from tension to calmness. The road hadn't changed, but I had. The Stoic exercise of focusing on what I could control – not the road, but my mind – was a powerful antidote to the anxiety I had initially felt.

Here are a few Stoic-based exercises to practise when you feel anxiety creeping in:

1. Progressive Muscle Relaxation (PMR)

- *How it works:* Combine deep breathing with progressive muscle relaxation. This method helps to release tension from the body and calm the nervous system.

- *How to do it:* Take a deep breath in, tense a group of muscles (e.g. your fists or your shoulders) for 5–10 seconds, then release the tension while exhaling. Move through different muscle groups in the body.

2. "4-7-8" Breathing

- *How it works:* This technique is based on controlling the length of your breath, helping to regulate the body's stress response.

- *How to do it:* Inhale quietly through your nose for 4 counts, hold the breath for 7 counts, then exhale completely through your mouth for 8 counts. Repeat the cycle 3 to 4 times.

3: Reflect and Gain Perspective

Ask yourself:

- Is what I am anxious about within my control?

- Which of the four Stoic virtues can guide me in this moment: Wisdom, Courage, Justice, or Temperance?

- Will what I'm anxious about matter in a month from now?

4: Reframe and Reflect

Choose one of the following quotes and say it out loud on your longest exhale:

"We suffer more in imagination than in reality." (Seneca)

"You have power over your mind, not outside events. Realise this, and you will find strength." (Marcus Aurelius)

"It's not things themselves that disturb us, but our opinions about them." (Epictetus)

"Do not let the future disturb you." (Marcus Aurelius)

Let these words help reframe your thoughts and ease your anxiety.

5: Change what you're doing

Take one small, grounding action to change your feeling state. Even a small thing like taking a brisk walk, having a shower or having a drink of water can help. A simple task brings you back to the present moment.

Riding and life: A mind game

Motorcycling, like life, is a mental game. Your mindset shapes your experience (more about this later). When you ride, you control your focus, your reactions, and your attitude. A ride made tough because of rain, wind, the terrain, traffic or fatigue can be miserable. Or it can be an exhilarating test of resilience. It's often both (yet another paradox). You decide how you experience it.

On the bike, you become both rider and observer, conscious of your fear, your decisions, your breath. This ability to observe ourselves is the beginning of self-mastery, and for many, it's a doorway to something greater than the ego.

Challenges, both on the road and in life, are inevitable. You can either fight them, resist them, complain about them, or you can lean in, adjust your approach, and find the rhythm. A twisty road demands your attention, your presence, and your willingness to focus and adapt. So does life. Riding teaches you that you are in control – not of the world but of yourself and your machine. You can't choose the weather, the road conditions or the actions of others, but you can choose how you respond.

The journey *is* the destination

For non-riders, the journey is usually something to endure, a means to get somewhere else. The real experience starts when they arrive. For us motorcyclists, the ride is the experience. Ewan McGregor and Charley Boorman, in their *Long Way Round and Long Way Down* adventures, epitomised this spirit. They could have taken a plane to their destinations, but anyone can do that! Instead, they chose the long, unpredictable path across continents with tough terrain – on two wheels. As McGregor put it, "When you're on a motorcycle, the journey is never just about getting from A to B. It's about everything in between."

Everything in between. That's where life happens. It's where full engagement brings joy. Unexpected stops, small towns, breakdowns, the people you meet along the way. The beauty isn't just in reaching the destination - it's also in the struggle, the challenge, the adventure of getting there. Just like in other areas of life, I have learned more and created more lasting memories from when things have gone wrong on a ride than when they have gone perfectly.

The risk, and why it's worth it

Motorcycling is risky. That's undeniable. Life itself is full of risks, and those risks are part of what makes it meaningful. As riders, we accept the danger not out of recklessness but because we understand the fundamental truth that safety is not the same as living. It's easy to trade in aliveness, joy and spontaneity for security. A safe and easy ride is good sometimes, but overall, I choose the challenging road.

We ride knowing that every journey requires focus, skill and awareness. That's the trade-off. The reward? A heightened sense of being alive. As Boorman said: "The world is meant to be experienced with the wind in your face and the hum of an engine beneath you."

And so, we ride. Not to escape life, but to meet it fully. Not because it's easy or safe, but because it's real. We ride because in a world that constantly tries to smooth out the bumps, we prefer to feel every twist and turn. Maybe motorcycling is a kind of madness. But if it is, it's one we wouldn't trade for anything.

Wind in our faces, hearts in our throats, souls wide open. That's not madness. It's freedom.

Chapter 2:

PLANNING, ANXIETY AND THE CHATTER IN OUR HEAD

The power of planning

I'm packed. The bike's been serviced and fitted with new tyres. It's clean, too. I always start a trip with a clean bike. I'm ready to ride.

The next morning, the world greets me with a beautiful spring day. I know exactly where I'm headed, not just today but for the next twenty-eight days. Every leg of the journey has been planned in detail. But why? Why spend hours over the past few weeks mapping routes, booking motels and planning "must-see" stops? I could have just jumped on the bike and gone wherever the road took me. I've done that before, so why do I choose to plan now?

I've been a touring motorcyclist for over fifty years, covering more than 800,000 kilometres across Australia, New Zealand and parts of Indonesia. That's like circling the earth twenty times! When I started doing touring trips, I'd set off wearing an old leather jacket, a map in my pocket, a bag strapped to the back seat with basic Occy Straps, and a somewhat vague idea of where I was headed. No reservations, but full of expectation and excitement.

I still feel that excitement, but experience has taught me something vital: a little planning can mean the difference between an unforgettable journey and a frustrating ordeal. Some riders argue that planning kills the spirit of adventure. I disagree. Planning doesn't limit freedom; it enables it. When I know the basics have been covered, I'm free to enjoy the ride, embrace detours, and respond to whatever the road throws at me.

The Stoics, who were known for their emphasis on preparation and rationality, offer valuable insights into planning. The saying "Luck is what happens when preparation meets opportunity" has been attributed to Seneca. Planning doesn't require rigid constraints; rather, it creates opportunities for success. People thrive when they have meaningful projects to work toward, particularly ones they are passionate about.

Another saying, often attributed to Benjamin Franklin, is relevant: "By failing to prepare, you are preparing to fail." Planning is about clarity, not control. It removes avoidable stress so you can fully immerse yourself in the joy of riding. Done properly, planning allows for flexibility, spontaneity and wonder, without chaos. You plan not to eliminate all risks but, rather, to reduce unnecessary ones. A well-planned trip ensures you don't miss what matters. There's always room for detours, surprises and spontaneity, whether it's a scenic mountain pass, a motorcycle museum or a local bakery famous for its pies.

But there's another hidden benefit to planning that often gets overlooked: anticipation. Psychologist Jeroen Nawijn in the Netherlands found that simply planning a holiday boosted people's happiness for up to eight weeks before the trip. It wasn't just the holiday that lifted their mood; it was also the excitement of imagining what was ahead. He suggested that taking several shorter holiday breaks throughout the year is the most beneficial, as you will have something to look forward to several times in the year. When you plan, your brain releases dopamine, the chemical linked with motivation and reward, so every time you picture the trip, check off a booking, or trace your route on a map, there's a release of dopamine. In other words, the holiday starts long before the engine fires up. Planning breeds the anticipation and stretches out the joy, giving you a double return: the fun of the trip itself and the pleasure of looking forward to it.

Planning a bike trip helps me prioritise. Life is no different. Without a plan, it's easy to drift, and you can end up chasing distractions instead of pursuing fulfilment. A good plan creates the conditions to fully enjoy spontaneity rather than kill it.

On the road without a plan might mean running out of fuel in the middle of nowhere or arriving late in a town to find no beds left. I once pulled into Tooleybuc on the New South Wales and Victoria border at dusk, expecting to find accommodation like I had in the past, but a local construction boom had filled every room. I rode another fifty kilometres in fading light, wary of kangaroos the entire way, to find a bed in Balranald. Fatigue, fading light and wildlife are a poor mix. Being tired and frustrated at the end of the day is also not a good mix when on a motorcycle.

In life, a lack of planning leads to confusion about priorities, poor decisions and missed opportunities. It can mean financial instability, frustration, needless worry and a nagging sense that you're not getting where you want to go.

The dangers of hesitation and procrastination

Negative self-talk and self-doubt fuel each other, which in turn leads to indecision and procrastination. This can have serious consequences, especially on a motorcycle. Hesitation at the wrong moment, whether at a stop sign, negotiating a tight bend or when overtaking a slow-moving truck, can put you in real danger. Many people think of procrastination as laziness or poor time management, but it's an active choice to delay what needs to be done out of fear or doubt. Whether on the road or in life, hesitation at the wrong moment can mean the difference between success and failure, or even safety and danger.

But even the best plans don't always work out.

It was September 2023. Ian and I were riding from my place in the Adelaide Hills across the Nullarbor to tour around Western Australia. As usual, I had spent time planning for this four-week, 7,500-kilometre ride. Mapping out routes, looking at touristy things, booking accommodation, and, most importantly, identifying fuel stops across the Nullarbor. Planning fuel stops isn't something I normally do, but crossing the 1,250-kilometre stretch of the Nullarbor Plains is different. Accounting for distance, speed and wind, I had calculated that we needed to fill up every 400 kilometres to be safe. I had mapped out our stops, so I felt confident.

Until we reached Mundrabilla.

We rolled into Mundrabilla Roadhouse with about sixty kilometres left in our tanks. Cutting it close, but still okay. A large sign came into view: FUEL. Relief!

Then I saw the small print: Only Diesel. The promise of fuel was soon dashed upon seeing the small crossed-out 'Unleaded' sign. My stomach sank. We had just sixty kilometres left in the tank. The next petrol station was 110 kilometres away. All my careful planning had just unravelled. We got off the bikes and went inside, unsure of what to do. After a tense twenty minutes, the manager disappeared out the back and returned with two 20-litre jerry cans. He wasn't sure if it was 91, 95, or 98 octane (we usually run 98), but at least it was petrol. We funnelled the fuel into our tanks, crossed our fingers, and set off again.

The lesson? Planning is essential, but not being wedded to your plan is just as important. Flexibility is vital. Sometimes, no matter how well you plan, life has other ideas and throws you a curveball. As many ancient philosophies such as Buddhism and the Stoics say, nothing is permanent. And the best laid plans are not immune to that principle. To think you can control things to fit your plans is an illusion. Embracing the "nothing is permanent" philosophy helps you be less stressed when your plans don't materalise as expected.

Touring, like life, is a dance between structure and flow. Planning gives you confidence, flexibility and freedom. In the words of General Dwight D. Eisenhower, Supreme Commander of the largest military invasion in history, "Plans are nothing; planning is everything." The process of planning clarifies your direction, your values and intentions and helps you prepare for uncertainty. In everyday life, and especially on a motorcycle trip, change and the need for flexibility are evident everywhere: changing weather, fleeting scenery, the ebb and flow of thoughts and moods. Embracing it allows us to ride through life more freely, without resisting what naturally comes and goes.

A plan gives purpose

In my late twenties, I realised I was drifting. No life plan, no real direction and no clear goals. Just working, eating, sleeping and repeating. It reminded me of Alice in *Alice in Wonderland* asking the Cheshire Cat which way she should go. When she says she doesn't care where, he replies, "Then it doesn't matter which way you go." This exchange illustrates perfectly why planning is essential. Without a clear destination, whether in life or on a motorcycling trip, we risk wandering aimlessly, facing unnecessary struggles and missing out on meaningful experiences.

Three years from now, you'll end up somewhere, but that shouldn't be left to the whims of chance. While "going with the flow" has its place, my experience coaching thousands of people has shown that having a plan with clear goals and benchmarks helps focus one's energy, sharpens decision-making, and leads to a far more fulfilling life. Think of high achievers in sports or business. Olympic athletes and successful businesses have plans, and they have been working those plans for years.

Planning helps manage risk. It encourages self-discipline, which I call the master key to success. With it, you can accomplish anything. Without it, nothing worthwhile or lasting can be achieved. Planning saves you time because you waste less time. It grounds your enthusiasm in practicality. And while not everything goes according to plan, it gives you something to come back to when things go off track.

How clear intention shapes outcomes

There's something deeper about the act of planning. It's not just an emotional and mental exercise; it's something deeper – some would say spiritual. When you take time to plan a journey or any other aspect of your life, you're doing more than logistics. You're making a declaration to the universe: "This matters." Planning expresses intentionality. And clear, deliberate intent is powerful. It shapes your attention, your actions, your perception and, perhaps, even your destiny. Planning channels your energy in a clear direction. Your clearly imagined path is a conscious collaboration with possibility.

I've come to believe that a ride begins not when the engine starts, but when the decision is made. A clear intention sets things in motion. In that sense, planning is a ritual – an aligning of will, awareness and desire. It's your way of telling the universe, "I'm ready." Motorcycle touring offers a perfect metaphor for life's balance: a structured plan gives you a base to stand on; the freedom of riding allows your spirit to roam. There's an old Islamic saying that goes something like, "Trust in Allah, but tie up your camel first." My version is "Trust yourself but pack your rain gear first." Choose your destination, but be open to detours.

In physics, there's a notion that the observer affects the outcome. Think of checking the pressure in a motorcycle tyre - you have to let a little air out to measure it, so the act of checking changes the thing you're measuring. That's the observer effect in everyday life. Planning a trip means choosing how you want to experience the world, which includes what terrain you'll traverse, what sights you'll see and what weather you might ride through. You are both shaping and being shaped by the journey you envisage.

The outer journey may be shaped by plans and detours, but the inner journey is steered by the voice we listen to most: our own. Sometimes offering guidance and wisdom, at other times being critical and judgemental, our self-talk plays a significant role in our mental and emotional well-being. Researchers at Harvard have found a strong link between anxiety and negative self-talk, while other research has suggested that positive self-talk increases confidence and happiness. Over time, I've recognised a part of my mind that engages in negative, cynical, sometimes catastrophising self-talk. My unwanted inner critic that points out my flaws, mistakes and shortcomings. I call it "Crocky," which is short for "Crocodile." Why? Because it lurks in the muddy waters of my subconscious, ready to strike at any moment.

Left unmanaged, Crocky discourages and chastises me and spreads fear and self-doubt. It is hostile not only to me, but it can also be critical of other people and the world at large. Remember, all this is happening inside my (sometimes very busy) head. Despite my decades of riding experience, Crocky occasionally makes me doubt myself on the bike. Crocky might say to me something like "This is a hard road; I might come off in these sharp bends". But I've learned that planning tames him. With proper preparation, I feel less fear and tension and more in control, and I'm able to focus on the ride. Stress, tension and anxiety are not your friends on a motorcycle. (They're not helpful in life, either.) When you're in control of a powerful machine, second-guessing yourself can be dangerous.

We all tell ourselves stories about who we are and how the world is. These self-narratives often stem from childhood and cultural conditioning and eventually shape our identity. To make sense of life, we all reach for labels: 'I am Australian', 'I am an engineer', 'I am a motorcyclist'. We wear these labels because they provide a sense of personal meaning, a life script to follow and a tribe to belong to. They also protect us, like a shell with armour, against uncertainty or attack and even from feeling the uncomfortable fact that our time on this planet is short. The risk is that by identifying too strongly with a label, it can provide an illusion of permanence in a world where nothing is permanent.

When we tell ourselves something often enough, we start to believe that it's true – that it's a fact. As an example, after a relationship breakup initiated by the other person, you might create a negative story in your head about being unlovable. The reality is this: just because one person doesn't love you, that doesn't mean you are unlovable. However, if you are continually hearing the negativity of Crocky, you will almost certainly feel worse. The most dangerous type of negative self-storytelling revolves around our perceptions of lovability and self-worth. Although these ruminations are simply confabulations or lies we tell ourselves, they often lead to a sense of helplessness and increase stress and anxiety.

A useful metaphor to illustrate the relationship between the conscious and subconscious is the relationship between a horse and its rider. The horse represents the subconscious mind, and the rider symbolises the conscious mind. It is relatively easy to train a horse to follow a certain trail. If you ride it repeatedly, the horse will learn the route and start following it instinctively. A novice rider is typically given the gentle horse that knows the route and forgives/ignores the novice's untrained actions. This translates to if you don't take control and let negative self-talk (Crocky) take hold, you may find yourself living a plodding life of routine and sameness, and where your self-talk comes true. If the novice wants to learn to take control, that will require training to be a better rider. Then they will be given horses to ride that are more responsive. This means that if you want something different and begin to 'rein in' your Crocky, you will begin to experience life in a new way. It takes time, but your life is waiting to respond to you. The accomplished rider can then be given a horse with a mind of its own, but which will respond to the instructions of an expert. Similarly, it is the job of the rider (our conscious mind) to train the horse (our subconscious) down a new track (into new patterns of thinking and behaviour). Left to its own devices, the horse will continue down the familiar path (even if that path leads to negativity and mediocrity).

The stories we tell ourselves shape our reality

Psychologists estimate that we have around 60,000 thoughts a day. These thoughts aren't isolated. They are "magnetic". Similar thoughts attract each other and cluster together to form the narratives we come to believe. The trouble is that we often mistake these mental stories for truth, forgetting they're just the mind's way of weaving a narrative. What we think about most builds into a template that will ultimately become our personal reality.

Each individual creates their own experience of the world through their beliefs, thoughts, emotions and expectations. But here's the good news: by identifying negative self-narratives and consciously rewriting them, we take back control – just like a skilled rider steering a horse onto a better trail.

Neuroscientists such as Nicole Vignola in her book *Rewire: Break the Cycle, Alter Your Thoughts and Create Lasting Change,* are showing scientifically that your brain isn't fixed – it's adaptable, and it continually reshapes itself by forming and pruning neural pathways. Every thought, habit and behaviour strengthens some circuits while weakening others. So, by changing your thoughts, habits and behaviour, it is possible to change your personal reality and experience of life.

More than once, I've faced long stretches of remote highway with limited fuel stops. "What if you run out of fuel?" or "What if you break down?" Crocky will whisper. But instead of giving in to worry, I remind myself that I have planned my routes carefully, refuelled at every reasonable opportunity, and, for some longer trips, I've carried small emergency fuel canisters. Preparation quieted the fear and turned it into confidence.

The best rides, like the best lives, are not the ones on which the unexpected never happens. They're the ones where the rider has prepared enough to enjoy it when it does. *The lessons I have learned on the bike – that preparation and perspective can transform fear into confidence – apply just as powerfully to our early experiences and the deeper stories we inherit from our families. While it's easier to tackle worries like fuel stops and bad weather, the real challenge lies in rewriting the stories that were written for us before we even knew how to ride.*

Let me share one of those stories. This one shaped the deepest parts of my life.

How a betrayal shaped my destiny

When my mother and father met each other for the first time, they were already in love. Mum had written to Dad for four years while he was a "guest" in a German prisoner-of-war camp, and their love had developed through that correspondence. One day in late 1945, he turned up unannounced, in uniform, at her front door in Stockport, England. A whirlwind six-week romance followed, despite her father's efforts to stop it.

Just before Dad was shipped back to Australia, he sent Mum a telegram: "Marry me or forget." I still have that telegram.

Mum chose love. They married in secret, and in January 1946, Mum arrived in Sydney as a war bride. She never saw her father again.

They planned to build a life together using Dad's four years of POW back pay. But that plan evaporated after he found that his sister had managed to get access to the funds. The money was gone. His sister's betrayal inflicted lasting wounds on top of his war trauma. Dad struggled with undiagnosed PTSD, and he lived with anxiety for the rest of his life.

So, they started with nothing. Dad painted houses, Mum raised two daughters. And seven years after my sister, I arrived.

The betrayal, mixed with my father's undiagnosed post-traumatic stress disorder, had taken place before I was born, but it laid the foundation of my childhood – and, in fact, my entire life. Financial stress. Emotional fragility. Isolation. We never met our cousins. There was no extended family support. We were on Struggle Street, and that street shaped everything: where we lived, the school I attended, the parenting I received.

As children, we absorb the emotional climate we grow up in. It shapes our self-talk and our beliefs about ourselves, others, and the world. By around age seven, we've formed most of our core beliefs. By then, an unconscious life script has been put in place that is designed to ensure survival and acceptance. Unless we pause to rewrite it, that script will run our lives.

My life script was written with ink from a difficult past. It was full of decisions about my worth, relationships and life expectations. I carried emotional baggage I didn't even know I had. I believed the world was harsh, that trust was dangerous, and that success was survival, not joy. I made unconscious decisions about who I was, what I deserved, and how safe it was to reach for more. And Crocky reinforced it all. That baggage lived in my nervous system. It whispered through my self-talk and shaped my choices.

Unresolved childhood wounds shape our adult relationships, too. We often choose partners who reflect the traits of our early caregivers, especially those traits that left us feeling unfulfilled or hurt. Psychotherapy teaches that we often subconsciously seek relationships that recreate those childhood wounds, not to suffer them again but as an unconscious attempt to heal them. But instead of healing, we often find ourselves stuck in cycles of conflict and misunderstanding.

How I rewrote my script and healed my childhood wounds

I was in my early twenties. After a traumatic breakup with my girlfriend, I came to see that I was riding through life on a type of blind autopilot. Hidden forces, old habits and patterns of behaviour, as well as unconscious fears and beliefs, were quietly but powerfully shaping my experience of life without me even realising it. At first, I couldn't name them, but I knew they were there. The first step in any genuine self-development is to shine a light into dark areas of yourself, so that those unconscious patterns and beliefs become conscious. After all, you cannot change something you don't even know exists. It is often comparable to gradually turning up the dimmer switch on the lights in your living room. The next step was harder – I had to commit to doing the work of change.

In the early 1980s, when the personal development industry was still in its infancy, a friend recommended to me a weekend-long, intense personal development workshop called The Turning Point. I signed up. At 6:30 p.m. on a Sunday in October 1982, I had an epiphany that changed my life. The epiphany was that I had to forgive my father for dying when I was just nine years old. What I discovered was that I had held on to bitterness, resentment and unresolved grief about him leaving me. This was exacerbated by the guilt I felt about the argument he and I had the night before he died. This proved to be the last time I ever saw him, and I felt deeply guilty about that. All this guilt, resentment and regret was what was holding me back in life.

I remember the time so precisely, because what happened next shaped the next 15 years of my life. I did all the Turning Point courses, trained as a facilitator, and went on to lead the program 155 times, helping thousands of Aussies and Kiwis experience their own personal breakthroughs.

Hungry to understand more, I dove into the world of psychology and self-development. Since that first workshop, I've read around 3,000 books on the subject. I worked with a Bioenergetic therapist for two years. That powerful therapy helped me unlock and heal deep emotional wounds that I hadn't known I'd been carrying. I have come to call this lifelong journey "Project Me". Over the years, I've invested more than $150,000 of my own money to attend countless workshops across Australia, New Zealand and the US. Some experiences were better than others, but I've never regretted a cent of the investment.

Not everyone needs to take the same path, but I believe everyone would benefit from doing the work of facing their past, breaking old patterns and consciously creating a new self.

Letting go of unnecessary baggage

Motorcyclists will often overpack, until they learn. Like most riders starting out, I used to take too much gear on the road. These days, whether I'm riding for four days or four months, I will take only what I need for five days. Because through trial and error, I've found that's enough. Extra weight makes the bike harder to handle, slower to respond, and more vulnerable to stress.

The same is true of emotional baggage. It slows you down. It makes life harder to steer. It weighs on your relationships, your confidence and your ability to experience joy.

As already mentioned, much of our baggage comes from childhood: the things we were told, the affection we did or didn't receive, the fear we internalised. Even if your childhood was mostly "good", there are subtle forms of conditioning that can often become beliefs. *I must earn love. I'm not good enough. I don't matter.* Such beliefs held as a child can shape adult behaviour. You will struggle to be your best self when you're burdened with emotional baggage. The voice of fear, negativity and doubt – your own Crocky – feeds on this. It tells you you're not ready. Not worthy. Not safe. But your Crocky isn't the truth talking to you; it's just the echo of old pain.

For example, perhaps someone who grew up with emotionally distant parents is drawn to partners who are unavailable or avoidant, which leads to a replaying of the same feelings of longing and rejection. They might unconsciously believe that if they can earn love from this type of person as an adult, it would finally heal the pain from their childhood. But unless both partners recognise the pattern and work towards conscious communication, the relationship can become a painful cycle of pursuing and distancing. Another example could be someone raised in a highly critical household who unconsciously chooses a partner who frequently points out their flaws. Although painful, the familiarity of criticism can feel to them like love, even though it erodes their self-esteem.

This pattern can also play out in motorcycling. Consider a rider who grew up feeling unrecognised or undervalued. Perhaps, as adults, they constantly seek to prove themselves. They may push themselves beyond their limits on the road, taking unnecessary risks to gain the validation they never received as a child. This could manifest in excessive speed, riding in unsafe conditions, or even choosing riding buddies who pressure them into reckless behaviour. Until they become aware of the deeper emotional drivers behind their choices, they may continue putting themselves in harm's way, mistaking adrenaline and external validation for self-worth.

Healing these patterns requires conscious awareness and intentional effort. By understanding these patterns, we can break free from destructive cycles and create relationships – whether they be romantic, at work, with friends, or with ourselves – that foster true growth, safety and connection.

The mind-body connection

Emotional baggage can also manifest physically. Unprocessed emotion and other psychological issues can get "lodged" in our bodies. We experience it as muscle tension. I have already introduced the American psychiatrist, Alexander Lowen. In the late 1970s, he founded Bioenergetics, a therapy based on the belief that there is a strong connection between the mind and the body. The basic premise of Bioenergetics and other somatic therapies is that the mind and the body are functionally identical. It links chronic muscular tension to past emotional and psychological issues and holds that by releasing the tension through specific body exercises and postures, a person can heal their physical and emotional problems. I know Bioenergetics works. I underwent two years of Bioenergetics therapy in the mid-1980s, and it changed my life. I also did some training in specific exercises in personal development workshops that I facilitated. Chronic muscle tightness isn't caused only by poor posture. It can also be due to frozen fear, grief or anger. Because your body remembers what your mind forgets.

Rewriting your story

I have covered how I rewrote my life script, but let's look at how to do it in a more general sense. The first step is to develop your inner witness.

Witness consciousness?

Witness consciousness, sometimes called the "observer self", is the ability to step back from the flow of your thoughts, emotions and experiences and simply observe them without judgement or attachment. It's like sitting in the stands rather than playing on the field, simply watching the game unfold rather than being carried away by every cheer, or every tackle or fend, or point scored. Just starting to observe your Crocky in action is the beginning of letting go of the control he has over you.

There is an important distinction to be made between your inner witness and Crocky. Unlike Crocky, your inner witness is a non-judgemental observer, whereas Crocky judges and criticises all the time. This practice of observing our thoughts and emotions helps us disentangle ourselves from our automatic reactions and gives us a spacious perspective on what's happening in our lives.

How to develop your inner witness

Developing this witness is key to self-development and personal freedom. Awareness is the first step towards change. Here are a few ways to help develop it:

1. *Mindfulness meditation*: A core practice for witness consciousness. Sit quietly and focus on your breath. Notice as thoughts, emotions and sensations arise and pass. The key is to observe them without getting swept away or trying to change them.

2. *Body awareness*: Pay attention like a curious scientist to the sensations in your body – for example, tightness, warmth, tingling, tension.

3. *Thought labelling*: When a thought arises, label it. Is it worrying, planning or judging? This simple step creates distance between you and the thought itself. Negative and/or fear or guilt-based thoughts tighten your muscles, narrow your focus and increase stress. Positive thoughts create space, softness and flow. The difference is immediate and physical. When riding, it's the difference between white-knuckling a tight corner and flowing through it with grace.

4. *Reflective journalling*: At the end of the day, write about your experiences, noting what happened and how you felt, but from a slightly detached perspective. Over time, this will strengthen your ability to observe rather than react.

Emotional baggage is also formed throughout life by unresolved trauma and/or painful experiences. These take many forms: the loss of a loved one through death or divorce, a major accident, a childhood health diagnosis. A betrayal. There are also emotions, for example, heartbreak or grief, which, if left unaddressed, will become burdens. All these things can (and often do) leave emotional scars.

Why bother developing witness consciousness?

"Not everything that is faced can be changed, but nothing can be changed until it is faced." These words by US civil rights activist James Baldwin sum up the first step to changing your negative self-talk into something more positive. You can't change if you are unaware that something needs to change. Self-awareness is the first step.

The witness allows you to step back and observe your thoughts, feelings and bodily sensations, helping you live more consciously in the moment. It helps you become increasingly aware of everything that shapes your actions. It allows you to align your behaviour with your values and your true self. When you're not present, you're unfocused, and your mind wanders from the task at hand. On a motorcycle, choosing to be conscious and fully present while riding can be a life-or-death decision.

The day I ignored the wobble

Early one morning, I set off on a solo ride through the Adelaide Hills. About twenty minutes in, I felt a slight wobble in the handlebars. It wasn't dramatic, just enough to be noticeable – a soft pulse that came and went. I ignored it. The ride was going beautifully, and I didn't want to interrupt the flow. But that inner voice, the "witness," kept tapping on my shoulder.

I pulled over.

The front tyre had dropped below safe pressure due to a slow leak from an embedded nail. Had I kept riding, I could have easily hit one of those sweeping bends with a compromised tyre and ended up in serious trouble.

The lesson

I chose to address the subtle signal that something wasn't right. If I'd chosen denial or distraction and pushed on, there would have been no change to an unsafe situation. That small act of awareness – choosing presence over autopilot – made all the difference.

Just like negative self-talk, signals from the witness are often subtle. A faint unease. A pattern you keep repeating. A discomfort in your gut. The motorcycle becomes the metaphor: if you ignore the wobble, consequences will eventually catch you. But when you become the witness – when you pause, observe, and choose action – you move from being a passenger in your life to taking the handlebars again.

Two kinds of thoughts

Basically, there are only two kinds of thoughts. They either constrict or expand. No surprises here: negative thoughts constrict us, and positive thoughts expand us. And you can feel the difference emotionally and physically. Positive self-talk is about choosing those thoughts that provide us a little more space to expand into. In contrast, Crocky is the apex predator or the negative thought food chain.

Research by American psychologist Angela Duckworth, best known for her work on "grit" – the combination of passion and perseverance – confirms that negative self-talk has a detrimental impact on resilience, motivation and long-term success. Other research has examined extensively the interconnectedness of thoughts, emotions, actions and outcomes, and has highlighted how our cognitive processes influence our feelings, our behaviour and our subsequent results.

In a nutshell, your self-talk matters. As a motorcyclist, it affects your riding. In life, it affects everything. Ultimately, it determines your character. You become what you think about most often. Every physical habit starts with a thought. Every physical "thing" started with a thought. Your life is a result of your thinking; so, to change your life, you must change your thinking.

The following diagram illustrates how our mindset influences our behaviour.

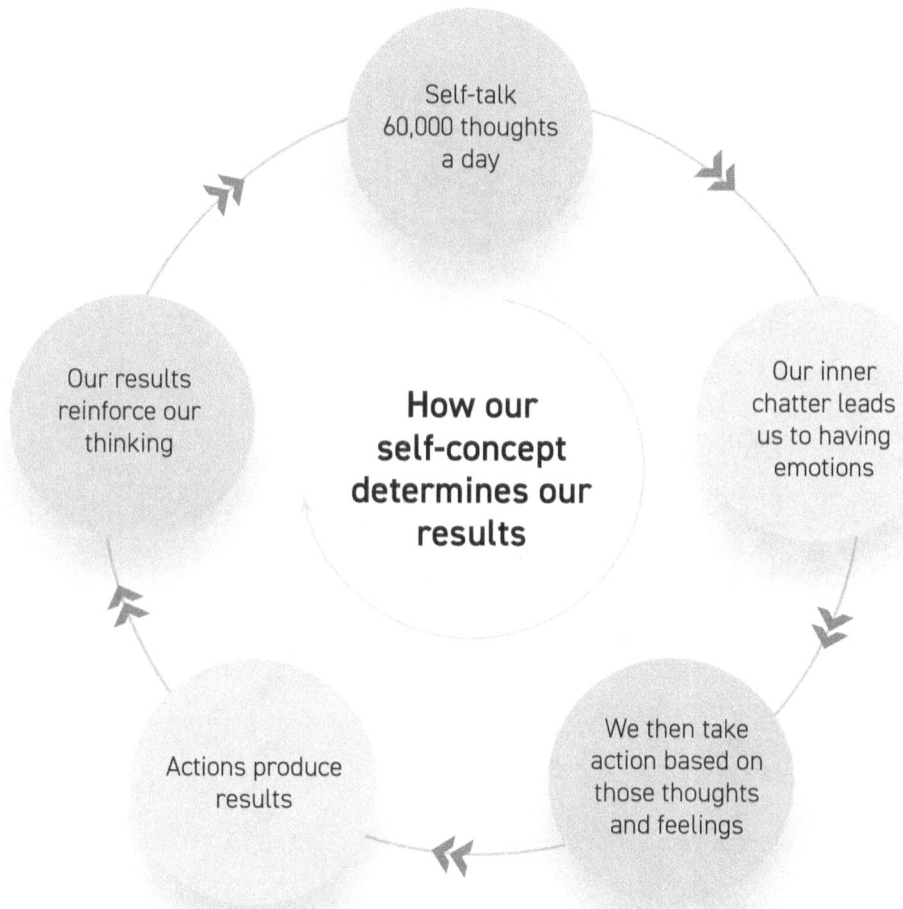

Five ways to control Crocky and overcome negative, self-defeating thoughts

1. *Plan with purpose*: As mentioned earlier, planning helps you focus on what truly matters – and what (or whom) to leave behind, including emotional baggage and negative people.

2. *Practice forgiveness*: Pry loose its grip on you and reclaim the inner road. As Christian author Lewis B. Smedes wrote, "To forgive is to set a prisoner free and discover that the prisoner was you." Holding on to resentment, blame or regret doesn't protect you; it imprisons you. It feeds *Crocky*, fuels negativity and creates blockages in your emotions, your energy, and even your body.

The *Oxford Dictionary* defines forgiveness as *"To give up a desire to punish; to cease feeling resentment toward, to pardon."* But forgiveness isn't about excusing the behaviour or pretending it didn't hurt. It is something you do to heal you, and it has little to do with the other person. It **releases you** from the grip of the past. It's an act of inner liberation – a conscious decision to stop carrying the emotional weight that's been slowing you down.

Forgiveness clears the road so you can move forward, lighter and freer.

- Reflective questions to help you understand whom you need to forgive:
- Whom do I need to forgive? (Am I one of them?)
- Am I willing to forgive them? (Myself?)
- What pain do I still carry?
- What resentment is weighing me down?
- Do I have any regrets?
- Do I feel guilt or shame about anything?
- Is there something I need to forgive myself for?

Also, try this:

Write the "thing" down. Note exactly what happened, how it affected you, and what you're willing to release. Being willing to forgive is the first step. Then, offer forgiveness – or ask for it – even silently. You're not making the past right. You're letting go so you can be free.

Above all, be kind to yourself. You wouldn't speak to a friend the way your Crocky sometimes speaks to you (if he's anything like mine). So, challenge that inner voice. Replace judgement with compassion. Let forgiveness be your way back to the open road.

Motorcycle metaphor: Forgiveness is like easing off the throttle after having clenched it too tightly for too long. You're not trying to re-ride the road behind you; you're simply releasing the tension from your gripping so you can ride ahead with more clarity, ease and peace.

3. *Embrace the power of a mindset of possibility.* Some people believe their abilities are fixed. That they are born with certain talents or limitations that cannot be changed. This belief becomes an invisible anchor that holds them back from exploring their full potential. They might think, *I'm just not good at this*, or *I've never been a natural at this*, but those sorts of thoughts lead to a mindset where challenges are seen as barriers rather than opportunities for growth.

But the truth is this: abilities are not static. They are malleable and can be shaped by our actions, effort and willingness to learn. Those who thrive know that skills and attitudes can be cultivated over time. When you adopt an expansive thinking and possibility mindset approach, over time, you will:

See setbacks not as failures but opportunities to learn and improve.

Approach challenges with resilience, knowing that each obstacle is a chance to grow stronger.

Commit to the principle of constant and never-ending improvement (CANI).

Change the way you view yourself, understanding that your potential is limitless and can expand with effort.

Cultivate curiosity about your limits and what it takes to push past them.

Trust in the process, knowing that growth is a journey, not a destination.

Celebrate the small wins, as each step forwards builds momentum for bigger progress.

Developing a mindset of possibility shifts your focus from what you can't do to what you *can* develop. You will know that with persistence and the right attitude, growth is always within reach. The goal is progress, not perfection.

> 4. *Choose the challenge path to tame Crocky*. One of the best ways to silence the negative self-talk of Crocky is by confronting challenges head on. We call this embracing *The Challenge Path*: a personal commitment to pushing through difficulties that demands effort, persistence and focus. Here's how to tackle it:

Select a challenge that stretches you (e.g. mastering a new skill or overcoming a mental block).

Stick with it for a set period, even when Crocky tells you to give up.

Draw your motivation from within; this is your intrinsic drive, and it's the key to overcoming Crocky's negativity.

Choosing *The Challenge Path* will bring up all kinds of self-doubt. Crocky will whisper, "You can't do it!" or "It's too hard!". But every time you keep going despite those thoughts, you build resilience and strengthen your self-belief.

A motorcycling example. Years ago, I faced one of the toughest motorcycling skills: tight, low-speed U-turns on a fully-laden touring bike. (For non-riders, these are way harder than they look.) This challenge required more than technique; it required patience, balance and a calm mind. Every part of me resisted. Crocky was loud: "You'll drop it! Everyone's watching! You're too old for this!"

But I made a commitment: ten minutes a day, for thirty days. I found a spot in an empty car park and showed up, rain or shine. I treated it like a meditation: each loop through the cones was a breath, and every mistake a reminder to return to the present.

Some days, I nailed it. Other days, I got frustrated and wanted to quit. I even dropped the bike twice. But I kept showing up. By week three, my turns got tighter, my body synced with the rhythm, and my mind found stillness in motion. Crocky's voice faded.

The real challenge wasn't the U-turns. It was the discipline to keep showing up. It wasn't about the bike. Rather, it was about mastering myself and overcoming Crocky. That's *The Challenge Path*, and that's how you tame the negative thoughts that hold you back.

5. *Be compassionate with yourself.* If we don't have compassion for ourselves, Crocky will lead us down a rabbit hole of negative, self-deprecating and dysfunctional self-talk, and endless ruminations on the negative. The wounds we carry become the raw material for our awakening. Emotional baggage is not a flaw; it's a teacher. It calls us inward. It urges us to heal, to awaken, to evolve.

In that sense, every struggle contains a hidden grace. The pain becomes the portal. The family wound becomes the forge.

And healing? Healing is letting go, but it's also remembering who you were before the wound.

Back to motorcycling

As mentioned earlier in Chapter 1, one of the motorcycling paradoxes is that riding creates stress and anxiety sometimes, but, overall, it has been one of my most important tools for handling stress and anxiety. Anxiety- and stress-provoking situations that I've personally experienced on two wheels include:

- Hitting gravel on a curve at speed and nearly losing control.
- Being hit on the helmet by a large bird.

- Dodging things that had fallen off a trailer in front of me.
- Riding through a deeper-than-expected pothole and nearly losing control.
- My back wheel sliding out on black ice.
- A car driving through a stop sign and nearly hitting me.
- A bee inside my helmet.
- Bright sunshine in my eyes making it almost impossible to see.
- The bike slipping out on a wet railway crossing.

These are just a few of the things that have happened to me over the decades that have caused some anxiety. Most are of no consequence when in a car, but they could be potentially catastrophic on a motorcycle.

When you're driving a car and come across the things listed above, you can often simply straddle the obstacles, because you have four wheels. It's not so easy on a bike, though, because, for example, hitting gravel at speed can lead to the bike becoming unstable. "Target fixation" describes what happens when you see an obstacle on the road, say a box of rubbish that has fallen from a trailer, and you focus on it – your eyes fix on it. It's a well-known fact among bikers that your bike will go where you look. Thus, if you're fixated on the obstacle, you're likely to ride straight into it.

When you have travelled through the countryside, no doubt, you will have seen markers on the side of the road or flowers on trees indicating sites where people have died. And often, you may have noticed that that tree is the only one in a hundred metres. There is every chance that the person who hit the tree suffered from target fixation. All they could see was the tree; the bike goes where you look; and *Bang!*

Life works the same way.

What you focus on, you move toward, whether consciously or unconsciously. If your thoughts are constantly fixed on what could go wrong, you'll start steering your life in that direction, just like a bike veering into the very obstacle its rider is trying to avoid.

Think about when someone is terrified of failing in a relationship. If all they focus on is not getting hurt or being abandoned, they will start acting in ways that are overly cautious, insecure or defensive – thus, ironically, pushing the other person away and creating the very outcome they have been fearing.

On a bike, if all you can see is the hazard, you'll probably hit it. But if you shift your focus to where you want to go, you can give yourself the best chance of getting there. This applies whether it's safely getting around a gravel patch or through a tough time in life.

The Stoic Emperor, Marcus Aurelius, advised, "You have power over your mind – not outside events. Realise this, and you will find strength." Planning is about controlling what we can while accepting that some things remain beyond our control. Good planning doesn't impose rigid constraints. Rather, it creates opportunities for success.

People thrive when they have a meaningful project to work towards. When planning a trip, you assess your riding skills, physical endurance and mechanical knowledge. Likewise, in life, self-reflection helps you identify strengths and areas for improvement. Having clarity about your capabilities enables you to navigate challenges more effectively.

However, if you focus too much on a problem, you can risk becoming an expert in the problem rather than in searching for a solution. That doesn't mean ignore your problem. Thoroughly diagnosing an issue is essential, but the key is to then shift from analysis to action. Life is full of unexpected challenges. Over the past five years, you may have faced financial hardship, lost someone close, been made redundant, got married or divorced, dealt with illness, or experienced a serious accident. (I've had most of these over the course of my life.) The list of possibilities is endless.

Whatever the challenge, the more you dwell on the problem without moving to action, the bigger it becomes.

One of Crocky's favourite dysfunctional statements is: "I'm not good enough." When it is repeated often enough, negative self-talk will embed itself into our consciousness, turning false beliefs from your life script into self-fulfilling prophecies. Conversely, the same principle applies to positive self-talk. The more encouraging and self-affirming your inner dialogue, the more your confidence and self-esteem will grow.

A last point about planning: Managing your budget effectively

In 1990, I had a "financial learning experience". My then-wife and I lost everything. We had to sell the house and car – and after that, we were still in $100,000 debt. How did this happen? As is the case for most people who find themselves in a situation like this, it was a mix of things. Some external factors, such as a struggling New Zealand economy, and some internal factors, in our case, a series of (what turned out to be) bad decisions. A major lesson that came out of that experience was that, whether you're planning a motorcycle trip or more generally in life, having a realistic budget allows you to set expectations and allocate your available funds wisely.

The road as a symbol of transformation

Every road trip you plot mirrors a journey within. Hills, valleys, coastlines, roadworks: these are outer forms of inner states. Selecting and planning for a remote stretch or a winding pass is more than geography; it's an invitation to stretch personal possibilities and meet a version of yourself you haven't yet encountered. Roadworks are symbolic of having to do some personal development. Some might even say that planning a ride is a spiritual act: you are selecting the terrain on which your next personal transformation will occur.

Planning as a path to freedom

A well-planned ride is like a well-designed life that leads to a well-lived life. You set goals and prepare for the road ahead, but you remain open to detours, opportunities and surprises. Because, as any seasoned rider knows, sometimes the best moments happen when you take an unexpected turn and discover something you never planned for.

So, as you ride forward in life, don't just ask, "Where am I going?" Ask yourself, "Am I ready for the unexpected?" or "What opportunities might arise that I haven't planned for?" or "If I failed to achieve my plan, what would be the most likely cause of my failure?"

Chapter 3

DECISIONS, DETOURS AND RISKS

July 2015. A sunny winter's morning. A mate (let's call him John) and I had met up at a local café to go for a ride through the backroads of the Adelaide Hills. About ten minutes into the ride, John came off his bike. He was a hundred metres in front of me, and I remember watching him bounce along the tarmac, with his bike sliding away from him. Speed wasn't a factor. Inattention wasn't a factor. John had simply taken a wide line through a soft, sweeping curve and had misjudged it. His front wheel had gone off the road and into the gravel, and he had lost control. Like many unplanned mishaps in life, it could happen to anyone on a bad day.

Down he went.

John was sixty-five years old. He didn't bounce along the road quite as smoothly as he would have done in his twenties. Just as I stopped to lend a hand, John jumped up to look for his bike, which had skidded, riderless, onto a soft patch of grass. When I asked him how he was, he simply said he was fine and fussed over his bike. I have had a few minor "come-offs" over the decades, plus I've helped others in this situation, so I was aware that adrenaline masks pain and can lead to a false sense of being uninjured. Thinking he was probably in shock and in adrenaline-filled denial, I tried my best to get him to sit down and take a breath, but he would have none of it. I wanted to call an ambulance, but he would have none of that, either.

By now, all non-motorcyclists reading this will be saying, "I knew it! Those things are dangerous. They're death traps! You'll never catch me on one of those things." (Yawn. We've heard it all before from naysayers who have likely never ridden at all.) Everyone has opinions. The trouble is that some people take their opinions as fact, not simply their view of things. Plus, people with strong opinions will often judge others who don't agree with them.

As the minutes passed, I remained unable to convince him to let me call an ambulance. (With hindsight, I should have just called one anyway.) Instead, he called a tow truck for his bike. After making the call to the tow truck company, John explained why he didn't want to call an ambulance. The adrenaline rush had been temporary. By this time, the pain was taking over.

Life involves risk

At its core, life is a series of risks. From the moment we take our first steps as a child, risking a fall for the reward of walking, we engage in an ongoing wobbling dance with uncertainty. Imagine a toddler falling twenty times while learning to walk, then sitting up and saying, "That's it! I'm done with this walking thing!" No, they don't do that. They keep falling and "failing" until they get it right.

It's great to "fall and fail" when the consequences aren't that significant. Every decision we make, from choosing what to wear for that important meeting to forging new relationships, carries the potential for both failure and success. And without risk of failure, there is no progress.

Expansion and contraction

Two opposing forces exist within each of us: expansion and contraction.

Expansion is the driving force of growth that moves us towards what is possible. DNA carries the blueprint of our potential, and the force of expansion moves us towards that potential, fuelled by courage, passion, enthusiasm and action. These are the very qualities that push us to take risks and stretch beyond our limits into new experiences and achievements. Expansion is the force that pushes us beyond inertia and our resistance to change, inertia being the tendency for an object (or person) to remain either unmoving or in its current state of motion. Without expansion, nothing changes. However, if expansion dominates, it will lead to chaos: an overblown self-image, inappropriate risk-taking, and overly assertive, even aggressive, behaviour.

In Taoist philosophy, expansion is the Yang – the dynamic, outwards-moving energy that needs to be balanced. Left unchecked, expansion can lead to burnout or even self-destructive behaviour. The counterforce needed to balance it comes from the force of contraction, the Yin, which slows the expansion to a sustainable pace. It also can provide stability, patience and reflection. This aligns with the Stoic idea of control and acceptance: we must push forwards but also recognise limits.

Contraction can be fuelled by fear, shame, self-judgement and guilt – and Crocky. There are times when each of these – fear, shame, self-judgement and guilt – can be beneficial and lead to growth. For instance, fear can take you, fast, out of a dangerous situation. Shame can be a catalyst for change when one sees the consequences of one's negative actions. Self-judgement may be good for self-understanding (as long as it's not too judgemental). And guilt can be good if it results in acknowledgement of wrongdoing and provokes the desire to make things right and change for the better. However, fear can also be experienced in the form of anxiety, worry or terror and it can trigger avoidance, procrastination and self-doubt. Contraction is the force that seeks a state of inertia – for things to stay the same as they are.

When the negative aspects of fear, shame, judgement and guilt are in control, people tend to:

- Undervalue or belittle significant relationships.
- Procrastinate.
- Underachieve.
- Have lower self-esteem.
- Become indecisive and hesitant to avoid making mistakes.
- Judge others and belittle their successes.

- Stay in their comfort zones.
- Resist change.

At an extreme, fear will paralyse you. Psychologists tell us that fear plays a significant role in many mental health disorders, particularly anxiety disorders and phobias.

A Zen perspective: Expansion, contraction, and the Middle Way

Zen teaches that true mastery comes not from choosing between expansion or contraction but from moving fluidly between them. Zen also embraces the Middle Way of not overextending (which leads to suffering) and not resisting growth (which leads to stagnation). This means:

- Expansion must be done with awareness. Striving too aggressively creates suffering. As it is for a tree, growth happens naturally when conditions allow – not through force.

- Contraction must not become avoidance. Retreating from fear is not the same as mindful stillness. True stillness is an active state, a conscious choice rather than an unconscious reaction.

- Balance is dynamic, not static. Just as motorcyclist constantly adjust their balance when riding, we all must shift between expansion and contraction in response to life's conditions.

Ultimately, for personal growth to occur and to live more of our potential, expansion must outweigh contraction. Growth requires embracing expansion but doing so with mindfulness. Not by eliminating fear, because fear is part of the package of being human, but by acting despite fear. True growth moves in harmony with the moment; it's not about force or resistance. It balances bold action with mindful presence. The key is balance. Push forward with courage but remain grounded with awareness. That is the art of sustainable growth.

There's a risk in everything

Every action and decision – and even inaction – carries some level of uncertainty and potential for loss or harm. Whether crossing the street, making a career change, starting a relationship, or pursuing personal dreams, risk is always present. The key is not to eliminate risk – which is an impossible task, and how boring life would be if we could – but, rather, to understand, manage and sometimes embrace it as a necessary component of growth and fulfilment.

Imagine a life without risk. It would be safe, predictable and comfortable but also stagnant, dull and boring. Growth requires stepping beyond the familiar, embracing challenges and daring to move forward despite the apprehension that uncertainty brings. History is filled with examples of individuals who took risks and changed the world. Explorers who sailed into the unknown, inventors who defied conventional wisdom, and leaders who challenged the status quo. Their courage didn't guarantee success, but without it, they would have never discovered new horizons.

Appropriate or calculated risk isn't recklessness. It's calculated courage. Whether it's taking a leap in your career, pursuing a passion, opening a new business or simply trusting yourself to handle life's uncertainties, embracing risk is the gateway to growth. The greatest rewards in life, such as achievement, love, adventure and wisdom, are found on the other side of uncertainty. Life involves risk, not as an obstacle but a necessary ingredient in the pursuit of fulfilment.

Rosa Parks took a huge risk

Rosa Parks wasn't the first person to resist racial segregation, but she became a symbol of the American civil rights movement when she refused to give up her seat to a white passenger on a segregated bus in Montgomery, Alabama. This simple act of defiance brought enormous personal risk, as she faced arrest, threats, and the potential loss of her livelihood. Yet her courage sparked the Montgomery Bus Boycott, a movement that lasted for over a year and, ultimately, led to the desegregation of public transportation in the US. I doubt she got up on the morning of 1 December 1955 and thought, "I think I'll change the world today." But her willingness to take a stand against injustice, despite the dangers, helped change the course of American history and inspired generations to fight for equality.

And what about the Wright brothers?

Orville and Wilbur Wright were entrepreneurial engineers and inventors, but they were not wealthy. They risked everything – their savings, their reputations, and even their lives – to achieve what many believed was impossible: human flight. As is typically the case when it comes to big ideas, most people were sceptical. Some thought they were insane. Leading scientists of the time dismissed the idea that powered, controlled flight was achievable. But despite multiple failures, injuries and public ridicule, the Wright brothers persisted.

On 17 December 1903, the *Wright Flyer* made history when Orville took it up for its first controlled flight at Kitty Hawk, North Carolina. The Wright brothers' courage to challenge conventional wisdom and embrace risk revolutionised transportation, global connectivity and, unfortunately, also warfare. Today, air travel is a cornerstone of modern civilisation – all because two bicycle mechanics dared to take a risk.

A more recent example of courageous risk-taking is Volodymyr Zelenskyy's refusal to flee Ukraine in 2022. When Russia launched a full-scale invasion of Ukraine in February 2022, President Zelenskyy was offered evacuation by the US. His now-famous reply – "The fight is here; I need ammunition, not a ride" – was a courageous decision in the face of real danger, and it also marked a pivotal moment in modern leadership.

"The fight is here."

Choosing to remain in Kyiv under direct threat of capture or assassination was not only symbolic but also extraordinarily risky. His nation faced overwhelming military force, uncertainty about Western support, and the possibility of complete collapse. But Zelenskyy's decision to stay galvanised Ukrainian resolve. It inspired both civilians and the military, strengthened international support, and reframed the narrative of the conflict from one of inevitable defeat to one of determined resistance. The risk he took paid off politically, and it also became a symbolic cry for freedom in the twenty-first century.

And then there's motorcycling

Motorcycling is a perfect metaphor for risk in life. Every ride involves uncertainty and so many things that could go wrong – road conditions, bad weather, breakdowns, not to mention the near impossible task of predicting other drivers' actions – but it also offers incredible rewards. Riders mitigate risk through a combination of continually improving their skills; maintaining situational awareness (for example, not riding in a car's blind spot); bike preparation; practising defensive riding; "ATGATT" (wearing all the gear all the time); wearing airbag jackets; and maintaining safe following distances. This parallels how people manage risk in life – by understanding, preparing for, and accepting it as part of the journey.

Yes, motorcycling *is* inherently risky. And yes, the statistics are sobering. In Australia, motorcyclists are roughly thirty times more likely to die in crashes than people in cars. That figure alone is enough for many to dismiss motorcycling as reckless. But what non-riders often overlook is that many motorcycle accidents are due to factors that have little to do with the inherent dangers of riding itself.

Consider the rider who isn't wearing a helmet or other proper protective gear, such as an airbag jacket. The likelihood of their sustaining severe injuries in a crash is drastically increased. Or the one who climbs onto their bike under the influence of alcohol or drugs. Hardly a recipe for sharp reflexes. Then there's the unlicensed rider, with no formal training, pushing a defect-ridden motorcycle beyond his skill level. When disaster strikes in these situations, the motorcycle is not to blame. Poor choices made well before the crash are the culprit.

Risk, when managed wisely, is not the enemy. A life without risks is a life half-lived. The key distinction is between calculated risk and recklessness. The former enriches life, pushing boundaries and expanding horizons. The latter disregards consequences and invites disaster. Motorcycling, like life itself, demands respect for the balance between a life with risks and wisely managing the risks that are encountered.

The power and nature of risk

Risk is woven into the fabric of life. It surrounds us. Sometimes visible, often hidden, but always present. To live fully is to engage with risk. Whether it's hopping onto a motorcycle, speaking your truth, investing in a dream, or opening your heart to someone, risk involves crossing the threshold between safety and possibility.

Taking risks requires boldness. It demands that you step beyond the familiar, confront your fears and embrace uncertainty. In doing so, you cultivate courage, develop character and build genuine confidence. Playing it safe may feel comfortable, but comfort alone rarely leads to meaning or fulfilment.

In psychology, risk-taking is closely tied to decision-making under uncertainty – a deeply human experience. Waiting until you have all the facts may feel like the prudent thing to do, but life is rarely patient enough for that. If you wait too long, the moment may pass. And, ironically, people will often overestimate imagined dangers while underestimating real threats.

Not all risks are created equal. There's such a thing as reckless abandon, but there's also calculated risk. That's where you assess the odds, consider the stakes, and decide if the potential rewards will be worth it. That's where growth lives.

Risk can take many forms:

- *Physical*: For example, riding a motorcycle, rock climbing, or even driving a car or crossing a busy road.

- *Emotional*: Speaking your truth, falling in love, breaking up, or letting go of the past.

- *Financial*: Starting a business, changing careers, or making a bold investment.

- *Social*: Challenging the status quo, standing up for your beliefs, or sharing a vulnerable story.

It was in my early twenties, but I still remember the first time I rode a twisting mountain pass I didn't know well. It was in Tasmania. The sky was brooding, the road wet, and every curve was blind. I had two choices: turn back to safer ground or lean in and trust my skills, my bike, and my instincts. I chose to lean in. That ride wasn't reckless; it was calculated. I adjusted my speed, stayed alert, scanned ahead, and kept a relaxed grip. But it was still a risk. And like most risks worth taking, it gave me more than just adrenaline. It gave me presence, perspective, and proof that I could navigate uncertainty and come out stronger for it.

Motorcycling teaches you that risk is not the enemy. Avoidance is. The bike won't corner by itself. You have to lean into the curve, even if you can't see what's around the bend. And isn't life the same? The magic happens when you engage the risk with awareness, preparation and commitment. Not when you avoid it.

That's the paradox: the moment you lean in is the moment you begin to let go of fear and doubt and needing to know exactly how it ends.

In that moment, you're truly alive.

Evolution and risk-taking

From an evolutionary perspective, risk-taking is wired into human behaviour. Early humans faced risks daily when hunting for food, defending against predators, and exploring unknown territories. Taking risks was simply a part of everyday survival, and those who managed the risks effectively had a survival advantage.

In more recent times, most of us don't face survival risks on a daily basis, but we still deal with risks in different forms. Crossing the road comes to mind.

As Jonathan Haidt highlights in *The Anxious Generation*, modern society (particularly parents) has become obsessed with safety, often at the expense of growth. This phenomenon, now termed "safetyism", reflects an overprotective mindset that seeks to shield young people from challenge and failure. Well-intentioned though it may be, such an approach can have unintended consequences. Avoiding risk fosters fragility and dependence.

One doesn't become more resilient by avoiding difficulty. Resilience is forged through experience, including setbacks and failures. Just as a muscle strengthens through resistance, our capacity for courage and perseverance grows when we face challenges head on.

Encouraging younger generations to take manageable risks where the stakes are low but the lessons are profound helps them develop confidence and adaptability – and a healthy relationship with failure. For example, allowing children to climb trees, navigate social conflicts, or take on responsibilities that stretch their capabilities fosters independence and self-efficacy. Similarly, in adulthood, taking calculated risks, whether switching careers, traveling alone, or starting a new venture, opens doors to personal and professional growth. Life's richest experiences often lie just beyond our fears. The question isn't whether risks should be taken but, rather, *which* risks are worth taking. True fulfilment comes not from avoiding uncertainty but embracing it, knowing that each challenge overcome will strengthen the foundation of who we are.

In today's Western world, "safetyism" has spiralled out of control. Children engage in far less outdoor, unsupervised play than they used to. Instead, they spend their time indoors, glued to screens. Yet it's through unstructured play that allows them to fall off seesaws, climb too high or misjudge jumps that kids develop critical life skills. Early, low-stakes risks teach them resilience, communication and problem-solving, and it gives them the confidence to handle bigger challenges later in life. A scraped knee today could prevent a paralysing fear of failure tomorrow.

I'm not advocating for reckless risk-taking, but don't let fear – especially fear about something you cannot control – drive your decision-making. Focus on what you can control. Don't stress about it if it's out of your control. Much of the time, the fear of risk is greater than the risk itself!

Cynics and naysayers, many of whom will have never ridden, are quick to declare that motorcycling is reckless and dangerous and that it inevitably leads to disaster. They fail to recognise that risk-taking, when approached wisely, often brings the greatest rewards: new experiences, deep joy and personal growth. The truth is, too many people are dead long before they physically die, living so cautiously that, as Pink Floyd once put it, they become comfortably numb.

Perhaps we all need to be more like Iluminada Fabroa of the Philippines.

At 82 years of age, most people are taking it easy in retirement. Not Iluminada Fabroa of Cavite. She is a living testament to the idea that age need not prevent you from doing the things you want to do. In December 2022, after a three-day climb, she became the oldest woman to summit Mt Apo, the highest mountain peak in the Philippines (elevation 2,954 metres). Then, in 2023, Fabroa went skydiving over the island of Siquijor.

One person's risk might be a walk in the park for another. It's personal. Well-trained and experienced skydivers probably don't see what they do as a big deal. Personally, I don't see the point of what they do – jumping out of a perfectly good plane! But that's just me. Taking calculated risks isn't being irresponsible, because you're not ignoring consequences or acting without preparation. No one skydives without checking their parachute beforehand. Only a fool treks up a serious mountain with no plan and no supplies.

The Stoic philosophers Seneca, Marcus Aurelius, and Epictetus never used the word "risk-taking", but their teachings emphasise the need to face uncertainty, embrace challenges, and act despite fear. In other words, taking risks. As a motorcyclist and a Life Coach with several decades of experience in both arenas, I believe that avoiding risk means sacrificing dreams, goals and aspirations and, thus, forsaking some of the thrill of being truly alive. It means lost opportunities, when the reality is we never know if those opportunities are going to come our way again. In other words, to risk nothing is the greatest risk of all.

To fully live, you must embrace risk. I know that one day I'll have to give up motorcycling, and I know that when I do give it up, I'll be losing more than just the ride. I'll miss the exhilaration, joy and deep camaraderie I've found along the way. And that, to me, will be a far greater loss than the ride itself.

Back to John on the day of the accident

John's accident, the lessons of risk, and why didn't he want to call an ambulance?

I had only known John for a couple of years at this stage. Our friendship was built around bikes and riding. I had never met his wife, but I knew one thing: she *hated* motorcycles. Like many non-riders, she saw them as death traps. In her eyes, motorcyclists were little more than temporary Australians. Her disdain for bikes ran so deep that John wasn't allowed to keep his motorcycle at home. Instead, he stored his Suzuki V-Strom in his son's garage, a twenty-minute drive from his home. Every time he went for a ride, he had to drive there, pick up the bike, and then return it at the end of the day.

Her hatred wasn't entirely random. About thirty years earlier, a *friend* of *a friend* (someone she didn't even know personally) had been in a motorcycle accident and had suffered serious leg injuries. That was enough to cement in her mind the view that all motorcycles were deadly. She made it clear to John that he rode against her wishes.

The result? When John crashed that day, he was too scared to call her and admit he had been injured. Instead, we called *my* wife. Miranda worked in the city, about forty-five minutes away. She immediately dropped everything and headed our way. By the time Miranda arrived, John's pain had escalated. It was clear he needed medical attention – *urgently*. But he refused to go to a hospital. Looking back, I should have insisted, but hindsight is always 20/20.

"Take me to my GP," said John. So that's what Miranda did. While they drove him to his doctor's clinic, I rode home, changed out of my riding gear, and jumped in my car to meet them. By the time I arrived, the GP had already taken one look at John and sent him straight to the X-ray department next door.

The results came back quickly. The GP immediately wanted to call an ambulance. And, still, John refused.

Despite my repeated attempts, he also refused to call his wife. She still had *no idea* what was happening. John wanted to go to a private hospital on the outskirts of Adelaide, so I drove him there. But as soon as he was assessed, an emergency nurse came over and said words that hit me like a freight train: "Because of your friend's multiple serious injuries, we have ordered an ambulance to take him to the Royal Adelaide Hospital."

Before I could blink, John had been loaded into an ambulance and was on his way. Multiple serious injuries? That wasn't what we had expected when we had picked him up off the road. No wonder the one Nurofen tablet that I had had on me hadn't relieved his pain!

In this seemingly minor crash, John had broken three ribs, fractured his collarbone and punctured a lung. (Cue the naysayers: "We told you so!"). His gear had done its job. He didn't have a single scratch on him. Three of the doctors commented on how amazing that was. But the impact of hitting the ground had caused significant internal damage.

When I arrived at the RAH, John had been admitted and given serious painkillers. And only then, after everything, did he call his wife.

John spent five days in hospital. When he was discharged, he had his bike repaired and then immediately sold it. He has never ridden again. Yet, to this day, he quietly admits to me (out of his wife's earshot) that he still misses it. His wife, however, is happy.

Life lessons from John's accident

John and his family were incredibly grateful for what Miranda and I had done that day. But we hadn't done anything special. We had simply done what anyone would *do* for a friend when they're in trouble. You stay. You help. You don't walk away. That's a personal standard of mine – an internal rule I live by.

We all have personal standards, but many people have never taken the time to define them. Through coaching thousands of people, I've learned that one of the keys to happiness is identifying and refining your standards. When you do that, you start demanding more of yourself. You stop tolerating mediocrity, whether from yourself or others.

The principles you live by create the world you live in. If you change the principles you live by, you will change your world. Living with these principles in mind so they become a backdrop to your decisions and behaviour will change your life. Happiness and fulfilment are not due to a stroke of luck. They are the result of how we live our lives, and that is heavily influenced by the principles we live by. Living in congruence with a set of consciously defined principles may not be easy; in fact, sometimes it will be challenging, but, ultimately, it is the path to fulfilment. I know, myself, that the clearer I became on my principles and the harder I worked to bring them into my daily life, the more difficult it became to behave out of alignment with them. When I do behave in some way out of alignment with these principles, I feel guilty and sometimes even have a physical response. Those reactions are signs for me to get back on track, back to principles.

Another key lesson: Preparation matters

From that day forward, I've always carried a first aid kit on my bike (and in my car). That single Nurofen tablet was not much help for John that day. I've never had to use the first aid kit for myself, but I've lost count of how many times I've used it to help others.

After John's crash, I also took a deep dive into impact protection for motorcyclists. Most riders wear gear designed to protect against *abrasion*, but what about impact? If you come off a motorcycle, you tend to slide, and that's when it's good to have abrasion protection. But what if you hit something as you're sliding? Hitting something – another vehicle, a tree, a safety barrier – is when you do real damage to your body. What protection is there? Motorcycle airbag vests and jackets. The latest innovation in motorcycle safety, these things function like the airbags in cars, except you're wearing them.

I was so impressed that I started a business importing them from France and spent four years as the national distributor. It was an incredible period of my life, combining my love of motorcycling with my passion for coaching and presenting. I travelled the country, riding my BMW to motorcycle clubs, expos and events to demonstrate how the gear worked. Then, after a few years, I decided to step away. I sold the distribution rights and returned to enjoying motorcycling purely for the love of it.

Motorcycling: The unexpected detour, and the risk I took

I was deep in the Victorian High Country, riding a route that I'd carefully planned even though I'd ridden it before – sealed roads, scenic bends (or twisties as bikers call them), and a well-timed fuel stop. But as I crested a ridge, I saw a "ROAD CLOSED" sign ahead. No warning. No detour marked. No easy way back.

My fuel gauge was flirting with empty. That wouldn't ordinarily have been a problem, because there was fuel further up the road. But now it was a problem. And just to make things more interesting, I had no mobile signal.

The options? Ride back a hundred kilometres and risk running out of fuel or take an unsealed track that I knew reconnected with the main road. I had no dirt-riding experience beyond the odd stretch of gravel road, but I knew standing there wouldn't get me to my destination. So, I took the risk.

The track was rough – gravel, ruts and steep descents. It was not meant for large road bikes. I also had to cross a creek where the water nearly came up to my foot pegs. My heart was pounding the whole time. I was definitely questioning my decision, but it was virtually impossible to turn around. Fear wasn't going to get me out of this situation. It was going to require focus, adaptability and sheer determination.

After an hour of wrestling the bike through terrain I was completely unprepared for, I emerged onto a sealed road. Battered and exhausted, but triumphant. The risk had paid off. As well as teach me about off-road skills, that detour also taught me resilience. It is also one of the reasons I now carry a PLB (Personal Locator Beacon) whenever I am on the bike.

Sometimes, when life throws you off your planned route, you have to *take* the unknown track and trust yourself to get through it.

Uncertainty: The gateway to personal growth

The unexpected detour may be inconvenient or frightening, but it often brings us the exact lesson we need for growth. That is, if we're open to seeing it. In many spiritual traditions, uncertainty is something to be embraced as the field of all possibilities. The deeper journey often begins when the road ahead disappears, literally or figuratively. Certainty may create comfort, but uncertainty awakens consciousness. It forces us to let go our control of ego and surrender to the unfolding of life.

The nature of risk

And, finally, perhaps the biggest lesson of all: even the best-laid plans can fall apart. All that John and I had planned for that sunny winter morning in 2015 was a ride, a nice lunch and good company. However, our day took an unexpected turn.

As a coach, I encourage people to plan. The topic is so important that I made it the focus of Chapter Two. Planning provides clarity and direction. It helps you define what you want, why you want it, and how to get it. But as John Lennon famously sang, "Life is what happens to you while you're busy making other plans."

A plan is a great tool, but it's not the destination. Life is unpredictable. The ability to adapt, learn from mistakes and make course corrections is far more valuable than rigidly clinging to a plan.

The blind corner: A metaphor for risk

Three of my favourite roads for day rides each contain a sharp blind bend – a bend whose exit you cannot see. Every rider has come across one of these, often on a mountain road. Just last week, I had a close call on one of these corners. Luckily, I knew the road well, so I was taking it more slowly than I otherwise might have. As I was leaning into the curve, a huge truck appeared from the other direction, taking up more than its share of road.

I had a split second to decide what to do. I could ease off the throttle and sit the bike up. I could slam on the brakes and try to stop completely.

Or I could speed up and quickly change my line to avoid the truck. And that's exactly what I did.

A risky manoeuvre?

Yes, but in that moment, the calculated risk I took was the safest choice I could have made. Speed was my friend that day. The truth is that in motorcycling (and life), you can't ride well (or live fully) if you don't embrace a level of uncertainty. We experienced riders know to scan ahead, position our bodies and commit. I weighed up my options in a split second and took a calculated risk.

It was an almost instant decision based on my experience, skill and trust. That's risk in its purest form. Not the absence of danger or fear, but the presence of choice.

In life, as on the road, you'll never have all the facts before you come to the turn. Wait too long, and the moment will be gone. Lean too late, and the consequences will be real. But learn to ride the unknown with awareness and courage, and you'll find progress and freedom.

The bottom line: risk and reward

To live a full life, you cannot eliminate risk. A life without risk is a life half-lived. Fear is often exaggerated. Most obstacles are opportunities in disguise. But here's the thing: risk is personal. What feels risky to me might feel like nothing to you. I might ride motorcycles, lead fire walks, or abseil down cliffs, but you'll never catch me jumping out of a perfectly good plane. The key is calculating the risk for you.

For motorcycling, I manage risk by doing such things as wearing the right gear, keeping my bike in top condition, and always letting my family know where I'm going and how long I'll be out.

But risk isn't just about physical danger. It's about stepping outside your comfort zone. If you only do what feels safe and familiar, you'll never grow. You'll never learn. You'll never truly live.

Once you accept risk as a part of life, you can take responsibility for it. You can prepare. You can manage it. But pretending risk doesn't exist? That's reckless. Trying to avoid risk? Boring and futile. It leads to carelessness and missed opportunities. Worse, it robs you of the excitement, adventure and thrill that come from embracing the unknown.

And that, perhaps, is the biggest risk of all.

Chapter 4:

MINDFULNESS AND EMOTIONAL INTELLIGENCE

Recently, I was riding solo through the Adelaide Hills near where I live, enjoying the scenery and riding with no particular destination in mind. The road was damp from overnight rain, and a mist hovered in the gullies around Woodside. It was one of those mornings when it just feels great to be alive and on a motorcycle.

Everything slowed down – not physically, but mentally. My mind was still and quiet. I was riding in silence, with no music or podcast going through my helmet. Just me, the bike and nature. I became hyper-aware of little things: the gentle turn of the throttle grip, the slight lean into bends and corners, the scent of wet eucalypt. Somehow, I was no longer watching the scene; I was *in* it. It was not a challenging ride; in fact, it was almost blissful. I wasn't thinking about problems, nor about yesterday or tomorrow. I was just there, fully present in the moment.

That is when I got it: that's what mindfulness feels like in the saddle.

Motorcycling is often described by riders as more than a mere mode of transport – it's a form of meditation in motion. On a motorcycle, you maintain focus and are in the present moment to a much greater extent than when you're in a car. When you're riding, you're either fully present or at risk. It's easy to have your awareness drift off when driving a car, because there are so many distractions. Also, you might be thinking about the past or the future and, therefore, not fully present or a hundred percent engaged in what you're supposed to be doing. There can be serious consequences when your awareness drifts while driving a car, but they can be far worse when you're on a motorbike. It just takes a one- or two-second lapse in awareness at freeway speed to find yourself riding into oncoming traffic or off the edge of the road and heading towards a tree.

What is mindfulness?

Mindfulness is not just a trend or a passing fad. It's been practised across the world for over 2,500 years to alleviate psychological suffering and enhance emotional well-being. Ancient wisdom traditions have long taught it and espoused its benefits, and now scientific research is validating it. Mindfulness, at its core, is the practice of non-judgementally and intentionally paying attention to the present moment. It is a kind of mental training that helps you cultivate awareness, become calmer and clarify your thinking, and it provides insight. It's no longer confined to monasteries, yoga mats or incense-scented rooms. For those of us who tour on two wheels, it is an everyday necessity and, often, a profound experience.

When a rider is fully engaged – balancing on two wheels, monitoring road conditions, sensing the engine's feedback – there is little room for mind-wandering or distraction. I've spoken with many motorcyclists over the years who find that riding can feel like meditation, providing mental clarity and stress relief – certainly not every ride, but common enough to comment. In fact, one popular saying amongst bikers is that "you never see a motorcycle parked outside a therapist's office," hinting at the widely held belief that riding is therapeutic.

The concept of mindful motorcycling has deep roots in the riding community's collective consciousness. Long before "mindfulness" became a buzzword, motorcyclists were extolling the almost *spiritual* experience of a good ride. In *Zen and the Art of Motorcycle Maintenance*, Pirsig captured this sentiment by portraying motorcycle travel as an immersive, present-centered journey: "You're completely in contact with it all. You're in the scene, not just watching it, and the sense of presence is overwhelming." That overwhelming presence is essentially mindfulness – a total absorption in *here and now* that many riders know well.

Mindfulness is the art of being aware of but not trying to change your breathing, the gentle rise and fall of your chest, other bodily sensations, your thoughts, or your environment. It is riding with all your senses awake and all your attention engaged. On a motorcycle, this is not only ideal; it's vital. Mindfulness is a way of being, as well as a state of mind. And when you're riding a winding mountain road or threading a sweeping coastal curve, it's the difference between skimming the surface of life or diving deeply into it.

When meditation and mindfulness became "normal"

In 1967, when the Beatles publicly embraced Transcendental Meditation after attending a seminar by Maharishi Mahesh Yogi, the growth in the popularity of meditation in the West began to accelerate. In my career in professional and personal development, I've taught mindfulness and meditation techniques to thousands of people across Australia and New Zealand. The effects that I observed in those sessions – participants experiencing greater calmness, sharper focus, enhanced insight and deeper emotional resilience – have since been confirmed by a wealth of scientific research as typical outcomes of mindfulness and meditation.

Over the past thirty years, mindfulness and meditation have been the subjects of hundreds of studies. One *Harvard Business Review* study, for example, reported that mindfulness enhanced leadership by improving empathy, clarity and decision-making. Other studies consistently show reductions in stress and anxiety, improved concentration, and stronger overall well-being. Studies in the UK have found a clear link between mindfulness and a lower incidence of risky driving behaviour and fewer crashes.

These positive effects are beneficial at work or in relationships – and they're also vital on a motorcycle. On one ride, a kangaroo suddenly came into view and hopped across the road in front of me. Thanks to the mindfulness I'd cultivated over years, I didn't panic. I stayed calm, responded quickly but deliberately, and avoided a crash. That kind of presence – the ability to respond rather than react – is exactly what mindfulness helps develop.

On a deeper level, mindfulness connects us with the current moment, which is all we ever truly have. Riding a motorcycle makes this beautifully clear. The past is gone; the future is uncertain; but the curve you're in right now demands your full attention. In that sense, mindfulness is a way of riding. And a way of living. It's being present in the moment, not allowing your mind to wander. From the way we engage with our work to how we navigate personal relationships and even the way we play and ride, mindfulness has the power to enhance every experience.

The world of motorcycling is a great metaphor for mindfulness.

The mental health benefits of mindful riding

As well as demanding that you be present, focused, and have all your senses alert so you can keep your reactions sharp, mindfulness also helps you stay mentally and emotionally balanced. This applies whether you're navigating a winding mountain road or dealing with the curveballs life throws your way. Because when you're on two wheels, being present is critical, not optional, many riders describe motorcycling as a kind of moving meditation. The hum of the engine almost becomes a mantra. The rhythm of the road, the awareness of your posture and grip – it all pulls you into the present moment. On a bike, zoning out can cost you dearly.

Riding can be a powerful stress-buster and mood-enhancer. The intense focus required tends to push aside intrusive worries and anxieties, enabling a mental reset. As one rider vividly described it in an online survey, "When you are on the bike, dialled in and riding on the edge, there are no intrusive thoughts, no rumination, no pain – just pure focus, concentration, adrenaline, and joy." This immersive, present-moment awareness is very similar to the state achieved in mindfulness meditation, and it has tangible mental health benefits. That same survey found riders often reported that long rides left them calmer and happier (for example, "...clears all the shit out of my head").

Mindful riding through the Snowy Mountains

It must have been the early 1990s, because I was riding a BMW R100RS on my solo ride through the beautiful Snowy Mountains of New South Wales. It was spring. Fields of yellow followed fields of purple, followed by fields of luscious green. Beautiful. Back at home, I had been dealing with more than the usual amount of clutter of modern life. Work deadlines, family obligations, and that emotional and mental fatigue that creeps in when you've been running too hard for too long. That is why I had packed the bike and headed out on my own in search of the long straights and fast curves of the Snowy Mountains.

As I wound my way through the mountain passes, something remarkable began to happen. My thoughts, which had up until then been darting around like noisy birds, gradually fell silent. Each twist of the throttle got my full attention. Scanning the road, leaning into bends, feeling the change in pavement texture beneath the tyres and the cool air on my face – I was totally in the moment. About halfway through the second day, I realised I hadn't thought about work or felt stress for hours. My mind was clear, alert and surprisingly light. It wasn't avoiding my problems. I had just been so deeply immersed in the ride that they had had no room to intrude. It was as if the wind had blown the dust out of my head.

That night, parked up in a Jindabyne motel, I felt something I hadn't felt in weeks: calm. Not the kind you fake with deep breaths or distractions, but the kind that settles in when you've truly let go.

Mindfulness and our emotions

Think back to the best boss you've ever had. What made them stand out? I've asked this question of hundreds of people, and the answers given have been remarkably consistent. Words such as "inspiring", "authentic", "calm", and "approachable" come up time and time again.

Now think of the worst boss you've had. What qualities defined them? You'll likely hear descriptors such as "arrogant", "reactive", "self-absorbed", "unavailable", or "indecisive".

But perhaps the more important question is this: How did each of these leaders make you feel?

Most of us feel more motivated, empowered and engaged when working with a leader who's emotionally grounded. Someone who is self-aware, composed, empathetic and steady under pressure. In contrast, working under someone who is unpredictable or defensive, or who has poor people skills or is unaware of the emotional impact their behaviour has on you, can feel draining and demoralising.

So, what separates the two?

It's rarely IQ or technical expertise that differentiate a good boss from a bad one. High intelligence and impressive résumés may help people land roles, but what distinguishes truly great leaders is something deeper: emotional intelligence. The capacity to recognise, regulate and express emotions while being attuned to those of others. Unfortunately, many people move through life believing that IQ is the only "smart" there is and that emotions are secondary to intellect. They think that emotions are things that simply "happen" to them, as if they're at the mercy of every passing feeling. As a result, they:

- Let emotions dictate their behaviour
- Feel trapped in their moods
- React impulsively, as if there's no alternative
- Allow minor irritations or past regrets to shape entire days, or lifetimes.

What if there was another way?

Both science and motorcycling offer insight. Neuroscience tells us that while the amygdala (the brain's threat detection centre) reacts automatically to perceived danger, the prefrontal cortex, the part responsible for reasoning, reflection and conscious choice, can override that reaction. But only if we pause long enough to engage it. Emotional intelligence, then, is not about never feeling triggered; it's about cultivating the space between impulse and response.

It's like coming into a blind corner on a mountain road. The inexperienced rider might panic and grab the brakes. The skilled rider, by contrast, stays calm, leans into the curve, and adjusts with presence and control. Emotions, like curves, are not the problem. How we handle them determines whether we crash or glide through.

When we develop emotional intelligence, we reclaim control by understanding emotions, not suppressing them; expressing them intentionally and appropriately; and having empathy towards ourselves and others. This is what great riders, leaders and thinkers all have in common: an awareness that emotions are not enemies to be fought or master's to be obeyed. Instead, they see them as signals, information that can be used as guides towards better decisions and a richer experience of life.

A motorcycling lesson in emotional control

It was a blue dual-cab ute. I was leaving my street when it happened. The ute came flying around the bend just before my street – far too fast. As I turned onto the road, he nearly collected me. He only just managed to miss me. But instead of slowing down, he blasted his horn, as if I'd done something wrong.

I was furious.

My heart was racing, my hands clenched the handlebars, and adrenaline surged through me. My first instinct? Chase him down and let him have it. I wanted to scream abuse at him for nearly killing me.

But I didn't. Instead, I took three deep breaths.

I rode for a few hundred metres, then pulled over. I got off my bike, let out something between a roar and a scream that was, luckily, muffled by my helmet, then walked for a hundred metres up the road and back. As I paced, I focused on creating a distance from my anger, concentrating on and calming my breathing, letting my body process the adrenaline that was coursing through my veins. After a few minutes, the anger faded. My heart rate slowed, my mind cleared, and I was ready to ride again, having left the incident behind.

That incident was a reminder to me of the importance of acknowledging what I'm feeling and, rather than reacting impulsively, taking control of my emotions. I had chosen to act in a way that reflected who I wanted to be, rather than reacting based on my immediate emotional response. Emotions are powerful, but we don't have to be ruled by them. Strong emotions can cloud our thinking and influence our decision-making. Had I acted on impulse, I would have probably escalated the situation, maybe even turned a near-miss into something far worse. Instead, by giving myself space to process my emotions, I let go of the need to dwell on my rage and reclaimed control.

Since Daniel Goleman published his groundbreaking book *Emotional Intelligence: Why It Can Matter More Than IQ* in 1995, the concept of EQ (emotional quotient; used as a measure of emotional intelligence) has been the subject of a lot of research and many books. As Goleman writes, "In a very real sense we have two minds, one that thinks and one that feels." Non-academics might describe it as making decisions with either our heads (IQ) or our hearts (EQ) – and sometimes from both. He, and many others since, recognised that a high IQ did not guarantee success. For instance, have you ever known someone who was very intelligent but lacked relationship and communication skills? It is usually a challenge to build any sort of meaningful relationship with that sort of person.

In our data-driven, fact-based and analytical society, the major emphasis has been on developing the intellect. Making financial and business decisions based on facts, data and strategy makes sense. There's no doubt that having a decent IQ helps you get ahead. However, to get to the next level of competency in business and life requires more than just IQ. It requires blending the factual, data-driven aspects of IQ with the competencies of EQ. EQ, not IQ, solves company morale and cultural problems, improves relationships and drives motivation.

Emotional intelligence might seem to be a corporate fad, but it's also a powerful tool on two wheels. Riders with a decent level of emotional intelligence aren't dominated by their moods. They know how they're feeling; they can feel it in their bodies; they manage it; and they stay tuned to what others are going through – especially on group rides.

Being angry on a motorbike is dangerous. The lesson here is easy: don't ride if you're really angry! Your rage will cloud your thinking, influence your decision-making and increase your risk-taking. Awareness of your emotional state is crucial in making ride/don't ride decisions. At different times, we all have demons, the parts of our conscious and subconscious minds that are hooked on negativity, rage or self-flagellating thoughts (remember Crocky?). Whenever you are experiencing these, don't ride.

A Rider on an Elephant

This ancient metaphor from Indian philosophy describes the relationship between the atman (the individual soul) and the body. In modern terms, think of the rider as your rational, conscious mind, and the elephant as your body and emotional impulses: powerful, instinctive and sometimes unpredictable.

The "rider on the elephant" symbolises the delicate balance between logic and emotion. The rider may hold the reins, but the elephant's cooperation is essential. No matter how strong the rider's intentions, if the elephant wants to veer off course, it usually wins. The same is true in life: our rational thoughts may aim to guide us, but our emotions will often take the lead.

When rider and elephant move together in harmony, they make steady progress. But when they're in conflict, the elephant's emotional power can easily override reason, leading to impulsive or self-defeating actions.

This metaphor offers a powerful illustration of emotional intelligence. If you want to influence the rider, start with the elephant. When the elephant is agitated, the rider can't function effectively. Logic alone won't persuade someone whose emotions are unsettled. That's why empathy, timing and emotional awareness are critical in communication. Reflect for a moment. How often have you relied solely on reason, ignoring the emotional state beneath the surface?

Of course, this doesn't mean we excuse harmful behaviour driven by emotion. Just as Indian tradition holds the rider accountable for the elephant's actions, we too must take responsibility for our emotional responses. The goal is not to suppress emotions but, rather, to learn to express them wisely. It's no coincidence that high emotional intelligence competencies are commonly found in top performers, whether in the workplace or sports – or even motorcycling. What were once dismissed as "soft skills" are now recognised as vital qualities for success.

The core competencies of emotional intelligence

Emotional intelligence is the ability to recognise, understand and manage your own emotions and to recognise, understand, and influence the emotions of others. The key competencies are typically outlined as follows:

1. **Self-Awareness**
   The ability to accurately recognise your emotions and understand how they influence your thoughts and behaviour. Self-aware individuals have a clear sense of their strengths, weaknesses, values and core beliefs. They can also see how their emotional states affect their interactions and decisions.

2. **Self-Regulation**
   Building on self-awareness, self-regulation is the ability to manage or

redirect disruptive emotions and impulses. It's about staying in control, remaining calm under pressure, and making thoughtful choices, even in emotionally charged situations.

3. **Motivation**
This refers to *intrinsic* motivation – being driven by internal goals, personal values, standards and principles or a deep sense of purpose, rather than external rewards such as money or status. People with high emotional intelligence are often deeply committed, resilient in the face of setbacks, and passionate about what they do.

4. **Empathy**
The capacity to understand and share the feelings of others. Empathy allows you to see the world through someone else's eyes. It helps you respond with compassion, navigate conflicts more smoothly, and strengthen relationships.

5. **Social Skills**
The ability to manage relationships effectively, whether in a workplace, family or motorcycle club. People with strong social skills excel at communication, influence, collaboration and conflict resolution. They know how to connect with others in ways that foster trust and cooperation.

6. **Relationship Management**
The art of building and maintaining positive, fulfilling relationships. This includes clear communication, resolving disagreements constructively, and inspiring or influencing others while keeping relationships strong, even in challenging circumstances.

THE COMPONENTS OF EMOTIONAL INTELLIGENCE

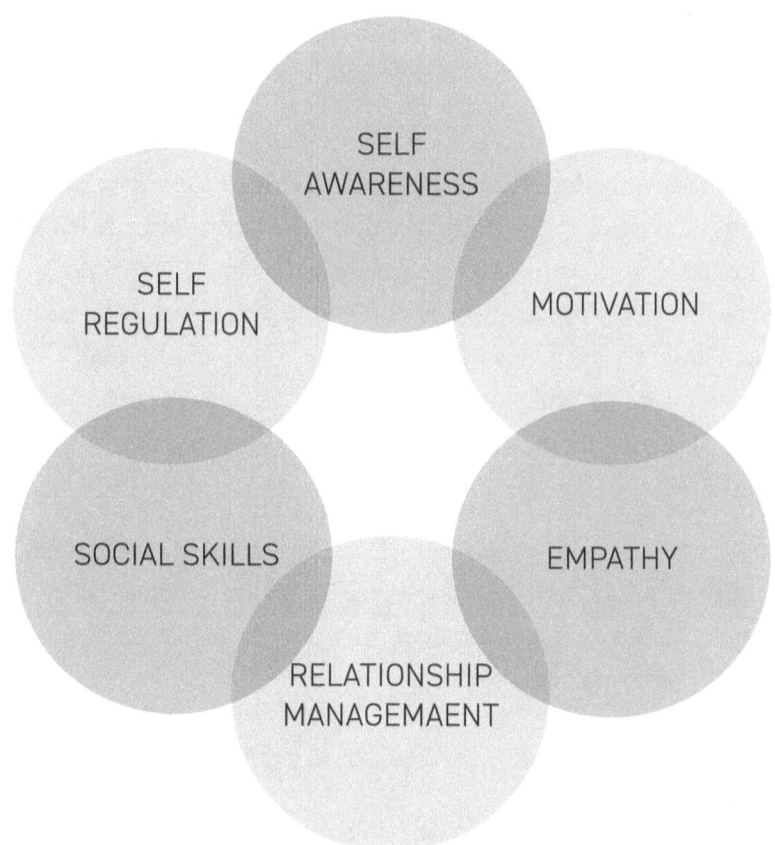

How a low-EQ day nearly cost us dearly

In the late 1970s, Ian and I attended the Castrol 6 Hour race at Amaroo Park, north of Sydney. For some reason, I was riding pillion on Ian's Yamaha XS1100. Somehow, we managed to find our way into a corporate area. And, of course, that meant free drinks. We were in our early twenties, and the prospect of free Guinness all day felt like a dream come true. We definitely made the most of it!

When it was time to leave, however, we were both more than a little drunk. In our haze, we forgot to call home to let our girlfriends know we'd be late. (This was long before the days of mobile phones.) But being young, full of testosterone, and feeling invincible, we thought nothing of it. In hindsight, we were far from invincible. We were being reckless.

Neither our IQs nor our EQs were active that day. After stumbling over to the bike, I honestly don't know how Ian managed to keep it upright, but, somehow, we set off in the gathering dark on the two-hour ride back to Ian's place at the base of the Blue Mountains. Looking back, it was an incredibly foolish decision. We were in the worst possible condition to be riding. And yet, we somehow made it home in one piece. Our actions could have had dire consequences. Natural selection had its chance to remove us from the gene pool, but it mustn't have been paying attention that day.

Our girlfriends didn't share our sense of triumph when we finally arrived. We got an earful about the dangers of riding under the influence. At the time, we didn't understand why they were so upset. After all, we'd made it home safely, hadn't we? But as I reflect on it now, I realise how young, dumb and incredibly lucky we were that day.

The internal witness

We all have internal voices that are constant companions. One of those voices is Crocky, our inner critic who judges, criticises and lays down the rules. An expert in catastrophising.

But remember that there's at least one other voice: the Witness. Calmly observing. Non-judgemental. Watchful. Detached. It watches without judging or reacting. The Witness might say, "Notice how tight your shoulders are", or "You're riding too fast for these conditions." Also, "I wonder what I can learn from this." It doesn't criticise or scold. It simply notices. That noticing creates a gap in time, and in that gap is the moment where choice lives.

How mindfulness and EQ are interconnected

1. Mindfulness helps develop your internal witness, and by doing that, it increases your self-awareness, which is an EQ competency. As a result, you're able to notice, understand and accept your emotions and bodily sensations better and make freer choices. This heightened awareness helps you identify emotional patterns before they hijack your behaviour.

2. When your self-awareness increases, this allows you to self-regulate or self-manage. Without self-awareness, you don't know what you need to manage.

3. Mindfulness deepens empathy and compassion. Research shows that regular mindfulness practice increases activity in the brain that is linked to empathy. As a result, you display more empathy and compassion and are more attuned to the needs of others.

4. Mindfulness enhances focus and motivation, which are both key traits of EQ. By cultivating moment-to-moment awareness, you're less likely to be hijacked by distractions or negative emotions. This clarity allows you to direct your energy where it matters most, stay committed to your goals, and respond to challenges with purpose rather than impulse.

5. Mindfulness promotes better relationship management through:

- Active listening
- Emotionally attuned communication
- Reduced conflict escalation.

Emotional rigidity, risk and control on the road

The Battleship, the Lighthouse, and the Ride Through the Unknown

One stormy night, a British battleship cut through the waves, its captain leading with experience and authority. Suddenly, the lookout called out, "Captain, there is a light bearing on our starboard bow!"

"Is it steady or moving?" asked the captain.

"Steady, sir."

That meant one thing: a direct collision course.

Without hesitation, the captain ordered his signal officer to send a message: "This is the captain of a British battleship. Alter your course 20 degrees to the south."

A response came: "Recommend you alter your course 20 degrees to the north."

The captain, irritated, insisted: "I am a captain in the Royal Navy. Alter your course immediately."

The reply followed: "I am a second-class seaman. You should alter your course."

Now furious, the captain sent his final command: "This is a battleship! Change your course immediately!"

After a brief pause, the last response arrived: "This is a lighthouse. Your call."

Reality didn't care about status, experience or authority. The captain had no choice but to adjust course or crash.

As in life in general, every motorcyclist will eventually face their own "lighthouse" moment – a time when emotional rigidity meets an unmovable reality. A rider who insists on taking a corner too fast because they think they can make it; who assumes the car at the intersection will see them; or who refuses to adjust to changing weather conditions is like a battleship steaming forward, blind to what lies ahead.

The road is the lighthouse. It won't move for you. *You* have to adjust, or you will face the consequences.

I've found that motorcycling is one of life's best teachers in this regard. Unlike driving in a car, which provides a greater degree of protection from the elements and from injury, riding a motorcycle offers immediate feedback. If you ignore reality, be it gravel on a turn, crosswinds on an open road, debris on the road or fatigue setting in, you will feel the consequences quickly. The best riders don't fight reality; they work with it.

Adventure riders, for example, Noraly Schoenmaker (a well-known rider known as Itchy Boots on YouTube), will often speak about staying calm under pressure, whether they're facing a border crossing, a flooded road, or a lonely night in a strange country. Their journeys are powered by mindset as much as horsepower.

Here are a few lessons from the Lighthouse.

1. Control what you can. Your gear, your line, your pace. Let go of what you can't control. The weather, traffic, roadblocks, the unexpected. You can work yourself into a neurotic mess by focusing on the wrong things.

2. "Stay present" is sometimes easier said than done. What's happening *now* is all that matters.

3. Remember to breathe. Many people breathe shallowly under stress. Take conscious, full breaths. Inhale through any stress and tension, exhale through stress.

Ecstasy, mindfulness and motorcycling

Ecstasy (or *ecstasis*) refers to a state of intense, transcendent joy, rapture or bliss that often transcends ordinary consciousness. In a more philosophical or spiritual context, ecstasy describes a state where an individual is overwhelmed by a feeling of oneness, heightened awareness or a profound connection to the universe, often leading to altered perceptions of self and reality. The term comes from the Greek word *ekstasis*, which means "standing outside oneself" or "being beside oneself". This suggests a state in which a person is so fully immersed in the present moment or experience that they feel detached from their usual, rational self, sometimes with a sense of losing personal boundaries. In some traditions, such as in certain religious or meditative practices, it's associated with mystical experiences or states of enlightenment.

Ecstasy can be both a profound, meaningful experience and a temporary state that arises from moments of intense beauty, creativity or spirituality. Some would say it's another way of describing mindfulness.

Ecstasy in motorcycling

For many experienced riders, particularly during long-distance tours or challenging rides, motorcycling demands that you be totally present and in the moment. In this state, time seems to fade away, and the rider becomes so connected to the bike and the road that there's no distinction between the self and the activity. As a rider navigates the curves of a mountain pass or feels the wind rush by, they may experience a deep sense of unity with the bike, becoming aware of every shift, every movement, as if the motorcycle were an extension of themselves.

Ecstasy can occur when a rider practices mindfulness, consciously paying attention to their senses (the sound of the engine, the feeling of the throttle, the scent of the air) while focusing on the task at hand. This full absorption in the act of riding can evoke an altered state of consciousness, much like meditation, where the mind is quiet and everything else falls away.

Mindfulness and ecstasy

In mindfulness, the goal is to be fully present, accepting each moment as it is, without judgement or distraction. When applied specifically to motorcycling – but it's also relevant in life – mindfulness involves:

1. *Focused attention*: When riding, a mindful rider pays full attention to their surroundings – the road, the engine sound, the bike's feedback, the sensation of motion – without distraction or attachment to past or future.

2. *Flow state*: When riders become immersed in the act of riding, they are in a state of "flow", where mental chatter quietens and time either slows down or disappears entirely. This moment of ecstasy can occur when the rider is so absorbed in the rhythm of the ride that they feel connected to something much larger than themselves.

3. *Presence in the moment*: A sense of ecstasy can arise when the rider lets go of everything except the current experience. It's the feeling of being completely alive, where every part of the journey, whether it's a sweeping bend or a quiet stretch of highway, is experienced with total clarity and focus.

In these moments, a rider transcends the ordinary, reaching a state where the mind is free and they are fully alive in the moment. It's a rare, often transformative experience where, much like meditation, the rider moves beyond just riding, they enter a state of *ecstasis* where both the ride and the mind seem to flow effortlessly together.

Summing up the traits of the mindful rider

As mentioned earlier, the traits of a mindful rider are deeply intertwined with both mindfulness and emotional intelligence. On the road, self-awareness is key; recognising when fear, overconfidence, or fatigue start to take hold allows a rider to adjust their approach. For many years, I thought this was the case, but now, researchers like Dr. Joe Dispenza, in his work on neuroplasticity, have shown that the act of becoming aware of our emotional and mental states rewires the brain, allowing us to make conscious choices rather than react out of habit. In life, this awareness translates into knowing your emotional state and understanding your triggers, which creates a foundation for better emotional management and personal growth. Self-regulation follows, whether it's easing off the throttle when frustration or nervousness arises or responding calmly during stressful situations in everyday life. By practicing emotional regulation, we can break free from the cycles of stress and anxiety that often govern our behaviour, ultimately creating a more balanced life – plus, you'll probably become a better rider.

Focus is another essential trait. On the bike, it means keeping your eyes ahead and your mind fully engaged. It means not zoning out but being present and mindful. When we are focused and present, we activate the parts of our brain that foster clarity, purpose and creativity. This same focus can be applied in life, ensuring that we remain attentive in work, relationships and conversations.

Adaptability is just as crucial. Riders will change pace or alter their route to suit shifting conditions. In life, adaptability reflects the ability to adjust gracefully to setbacks or unexpected changes. This kind of mental flexibility allows us to create new patterns of thought and behaviour, paving the way for lasting transformation. This is the importance of faking it till you become it. Practice enough faking of a particular trait and you're likely, over time, to rewire your brain and become what you've been faking.

Empathy is present when experienced riders offer support to those with less experience, mirroring the way we recognise and respond to the emotions of others with care in all aspects of life.

Presence, the ability to fully notice every shift and corner on the road, is equally applicable to life, where we seek to fully experience moments without distraction. This is the meaning of presence, or being in the present moment, and it is key to overcoming the automatic reactions that often come from living in the past or projecting into the future. Intentionality plays a significant role in both realms – choosing a riding line with purpose is a metaphor for living a life that aligns with one's personal values. The witness perspective, where we observe the road without judgement, is an example of the practice of observing thoughts without attachment – witnessing – allowing them to come and go freely, which enables greater mental clarity and emotional resilience.

Ultimately, mindfulness isn't simply clearing your mind or achieving perfect stillness. It's awareness, especially when it matters most. The more we become aware of our thoughts and emotions, the more we can begin to consciously shape our future. Riding provides a perfect environment for this kind of practice. Each journey is an opportunity to practice presence, emotional balance and self-awareness. Just as the throttle controls the bike, it mirrors the mind. The more intentional we are with both, the smoother the ride becomes. So, ride your ride, do it mindfully, and let each turn teach you something new about yourself.

Chapter 5:

THE PSYCHOLOGY OF FLOW: WHEN RIDER AND MACHINE BECOME ONE

Some rides you remember because something extraordinary happened: a mechanical failure, a breathtaking view, an unexpected storm, a surprising set of twisties, a dropped bike. And then there are rides you remember because nothing happened at all. No distractions, no effort, no awareness of time passing. Just you and the machine and the road blending into a single experience.

Ian and I were on a multi-week ride through country Victoria and south-western NSW. This is an area we've ridden many times over the years and is one of our favourite routes. After meeting at Halls Gap, we rode to Portland, then east along the Great Ocean Road, took the vehicle ferry from Queenscliff across to Sorrento, and then continued riding east across to one of my favourite bike roads, the Great Alpine Road and on up to Omeo. From there, we headed west to our pre-booked cottage in Harrietville. We took our time over four days to ride the 1,200 or so kilometres. It's a stunning region, full of great motorcycling roads and we'd booked the same cottage in Harrietville that we'd stayed at before.

After staying in Lakes Entrance for the night, we were on the road early and somewhere along the Great Alpine Road, between Omeo and Harrietville, the moment snuck up on me, as flow so often does. Something changed. Something clicked. This day started like any other ride. I ran my eye over the bike. I checked the tyres and my gear. Even though I knew it well, I double-checked the route and reviewed my mental checklist and then eased into the rhythm of the machine.

Flow Psychology: When the Rider and Machine Become One

At first, I was simply riding – adjusting my line, rolling on the throttle before I even consciously decided what to do. The road unfolded ahead, and I was just there, completely in it. The road curved ahead, snaking through rolling hills, and the pavement shimmered under the afternoon sun. I wasn't thinking about counter-steering or throttle control, yet every lean and acceleration felt effortless, almost perfect. My hands, feet and body worked in flawless harmony with the bike, without conscious thought. I wasn't riding the bike. I was simply "being the ride". I was, somehow, at one with the bike. In Buddhist metaphysics, *anatta* refers to the doctrine of "no self", the idea that our sense of a fixed, separate identity is an illusion. Flow experiences, especially those on a motorcycle, echo this. The self dissolves. There's no rider *doing* the riding. There's just riding.

That moment of pure connection got me thinking about what psychologists call flow – a state where thought and action merge seamlessly. A state that's central not just to peak performance but also to feeling deeply alive. Here's what flow is all about:

Flow is a state of complete immersion in an activity, where you're fully engaged, time feels distorted, and everything seems to click effortlessly.

Flow happens when your skills are perfectly matched to the challenge, creating a sense of deep focus and control. Mihaly Csikszentmihalyi, the Hungarian-American psychologist who pioneered the concept and co-founded the field of positive psychology, described flow as "an optimal state of consciousness where we feel our best and perform our best". It's often called an autotelic experience, essentially meaning the activity itself is the reward. You're doing it for the sheer joy of doing it.

In flow, the boundary between you and what you're doing dissolves. There's no rider riding. There's just the ride. Motorcyclists often describe it as the moment when the bike, the road and the rider become one, and everything feels perfectly aligned. That's flow.

On that ride to Harrietville, my focus wasn't forced, but it was absolute and complete. I was seeing everything: the changing textures of the road, the way the trees blurred at the edges of my vision, the subtle shift in wind pressure against my chest and the sun beating down on me. Every sense was alive. But none of it required effort. It just was. I wasn't thinking about braking, leaning, throttle control or negotiating the twisties. It all happened naturally. Each curve flowed seamlessly into the next, and I was completely absorbed in the moment. Time passed. I was so in the moment that I couldn't tell if it was minutes or hours. There was no clock in my head, no destination on my mind. There was only the ride. The usual distractions, the weight of daily life – emails left unanswered, bills I had to pay, what was for dinner – were all gone.

I don't remember the last hour of that ride. Not because I wasn't paying attention, but because I was paying attention to everything all at once. Time stretched and folded, and when, all of a sudden, I rolled into Harrietville, I felt a kind of calm that's hard to describe to those who've never experienced it. It's akin to what many spiritual and metaphysical traditions like Stoicism and Zen say about the present moment being the only real time there is.

When this happens, it feels as if the open road exists in a timeless dimension. If you've never had an experience of this nature, my challenge in describing it is like trying to describe what strawberries taste like to someone who has never even seen one. What I felt coming into Harrietville wasn't excitement or exhaustion. Just focus and clarity. The kind that only comes when the noise of life disappears, leaving only the pure, simple act of moving forward.

These moments on a motorcycle when the distinctions between rider, road, and machine dissolve are beyond thrilling. They are transcendent. In such moments, you ride untouched by stress or anxiety. This is the state of flow – a psychological experience, yes, but also a deeply metaphysical one.

Coming into Harrietville, I was in the zone. I experienced bliss. My sense of self had faded, and all that remained was the ride itself. And that, I real-

Flow Psychology: When the Rider and Machine Become One

ised, was why I rode. I was in a state of flow in which the act of riding had become a sort of "being" in itself.

Have you ever been so immersed in what you've been doing that time has just flown by? Have you had times when you were so focused that you were oblivious to the outside world, not noticing what was happening around you? Everyday concerns disappear. You're enjoying what you're doing. And things seem to be happening in slow motion. If so, you might have been experiencing flow.

You might call it being in the zone. You'll only know it has happened after it has happened. When we're in a flow state, we're so engrossed in what we're doing that it's almost as if nothing else exists. All of us have had such moments. Times when "everything clicks". Heightened focus and awareness. Confident in the moment and enjoying it. Our whole being is involved, and we're totally at one with our environment.

Csikszentmihalyi said this about flow: "The best moments in our lives are not the passive, receptive, relaxing times. The best moments usually occur if a person's body or mind is stretched to its limits in a voluntary effort to accomplish something difficult and worthwhile." Many touring riders report entering flow when riding long distances, especially on open roads with fast sweeping bends. The sort of roads where you can settle into a rhythm. There's a common theme amongst touring riders of repetition, immersion and solitude. The solitude aspect is exactly why, sometimes, for hours on end, I choose not to listen to anything in my helmet so that I can simply be with myself, the bike and the ride.

For other people, it might occur when playing sports or listening to music, or when they are totally absorbed in a project at work. Whatever it is, it's probably something in which the person has a degree of skill that has been built up over time.

In my professional life, I've done a lot of training and presenting, some 16,000 hours over about forty years. Some days I was ordinary. Many days I was good to excellent. But some days I was on fire. I was in the zone. I was in flow! Imagine you're giving a high-stakes presentation at work, something you've prepared for extensively. As you begin speaking, you feel completely engaged and certain of yourself because you are prepared and know your topic inside and out. Time seems to slow down, your words flow effortlessly, and you respond to questions with clarity and confidence. You're so immersed that you're not thinking about what comes next. Everything just clicks. The audience is engaged, and you walk away, afterwards realising that you had barely noticed the time passing. That's flow. Some might call it a mystical experience. In those times, I have been totally absorbed, I've lost all sense of time, and it's as if I've transcended myself and been "at one with the bike".

You might think my describing my "becoming-at-one-with-my-bike" as a mystical experience is a bit of an exaggeration. But is it? In his book *Bone Games: One Man's Search for the Ultimate Athletic High*, Rob Schultheis suggests that the mystical experiences that mountaineers have been known to experience could have something to do with the idea of flow. He linked "runner's high" with endorphins and several mood-boosting chemicals that researchers have found in people when they were in flow. I have spoken with other sportspeople – surfers, cyclists, skydivers, rock climbers and skiers – who have also had "mystical", flow-type experiences.

Riding a motorcycle, especially on long tours, is a perfect example of how flow can be experienced. When you're on the bike, you're engaged in a balance of physical and mental activities – controlling the throttle and brakes, shifting gears and navigating through the environment – all while staying aware of potential hazards such as inattentive drivers and road conditions. Riding requires focus, precision and a deep connection between mind and body – the very definition of flow.

Csikszentmihalyi described it as an *autotelic* experience—something you do simply because it feels good to do it. It's the kind of activity that challenges you just enough to keep you engaged without tipping into overwhelm, and the reward is built into the act itself. He suggested that you don't have to wait for this state to appear by chance—you can consciously invite it in, and in doing so, take charge of your own sense of happiness.

Why did Csikszentmihalyi use the term "flow"?

Csikszentmihalyi coined the term "flow" after surveying thousands of people from all walks of life, including businesspeople, artists, chess players, nomadic shepherds, musicians, surgeons and athletes. They all described peak experiences as moments when everything seemed to flow effortlessly. This was in the 1970s. It remains one of the largest studies on "optimal experiences" ever undertaken.

Can you make flow happen?

There are ways to make flow more likely. It is more likely to occur as an unintended side effect of doing something that you love and are skilled at doing. For instance, great musicians have often reported being in flow. Miles Davis, John Coltrane and jazz pianist Keith Jarrett described moments when they felt the music was simply flowing through them.

Motorcycling as a moving meditation in flow

Elite motorcycle racers are regularly in states of flow. Valentino Rossi, Marc Márquez and other MotoGP legends have often described races where they feel completely in the moment, reacting without thinking. In a post-race interview, Marc Márquez once said, "When I'm in the zone, everything seems to slow down. I stop thinking about braking points or apexes – it's like I can just see the track, and my body reacts automatically. If I start to overthink, I lose the rhythm. The best laps are the ones where I feel like I'm floating through the turns, completely in sync with the bike."

Similar to Márquez, Rossi often stated that during his most successful races, he entered a state in which everything felt effortless. For him, it was not just about the bike but also his deep connection with the road and the rhythm of the race. He noted that this often happened during critical moments in a race when his mind was focused entirely on the track, the bike and the other competitors. He described feeling a kind of automatic flow where every move felt precise, almost as though his body and the bike were moving in perfect harmony without any conscious effort. Rossi has said that this state occurred when he was in complete alignment with the bike's movements, almost as though it had become an extension of himself. His focus narrowed entirely on the next corner, adjusting his body position, throttle control and braking, all without conscious thought. The feedback from the bike, such as how the tires gripped or slid, became a part of his decision-making process. This fluidity and ability to adapt quickly were what defined his "flow" moments in racing. In an interview, he once said, "When I'm in the flow on a great road, it's like a dance. The bike and I move together, and everything else falls away. The sound of the engine, the feel of the tires gripping the pavement, the wind in my helmet – it all becomes a single experience, like being carried by the road itself." This is the classic merging of action and awareness that defines flow.

Flow in New Zealand

The South Island of New Zealand is a motorcycle dreamland. With my first wife as pillion, we were riding from Queenstown to Wanaka via the Crown Range Road, the highest sealed road in the country. We had only been living in New Zealand for a few months, and this was our first summer there. We didn't understand the weather in the South Island and didn't realise how cold it could be in summer. The sky was a beautiful blue, and the roads were fantastic, but it was so cold we had to buy extra gear to stay warm. There was almost zero traffic as we climbed steep switchbacks through alpine terrain, with clouds drifting beside us. It was cooler than what we were used to in January, but it wasn't freezing. On the descent, the road opened into wide sweeping bends, and we caught glimpses of Lake Wanaka far below. It was stunning. A magic day.

We both felt it.

We spoke about it afterwards. We had both been so focused on the road ahead that we had no longer been thinking about what we were doing. It was just happening. We were riding hard, but it felt like effortless coasting. Suddenly, everything had fallen away – our thoughts and plans and even our sense of self.

It was just us and the ride. We'd noticed the wind, the light filtering through tussock grass, the echo of the engine off granite. It wasn't adrenaline; it was awareness. A moving meditation in one of the world's most spectacular landscapes.

Recapping and expanding the key elements of flow

Earlier, I described moments of flow on the road experienced during those immersive, timeless rides when everything clicks. Here, I want to recap and then expand on the core elements of flow as they apply to motorcycling, and life more broadly.

1. *Intense and focused concentration on the present moment.* Flow requires deep, undivided attention. When in flow, distractions fall away, and all awareness is centred on the immediate task. The mind isn't wandering to the past or future. It's anchored fully in the now. You're so focused that there's no room in your mind for anything else. On a motorcycle, this shows up when you're scanning the road ahead, leaning into a curve, and responding moment to moment with full awareness.

2. *Merging of action and awareness.* You're no longer consciously thinking about what you're doing; you *are* the doing. There's a seamless integration between your intentions and your actions, like shifting gears without thinking or instinctively adjusting your line through a bend. The boundary between you and the activity fades, creating a sense of unity with the task at hand.

3. *A loss of reflective self-consciousness.* Crocky is silenced by flow. There's no inner critic or mental chatter about how you're being perceived, whether you're good enough, or what others might think. The judge-

mental inner voice that can cause hesitation or insecurity fades into silence. What's left is pure presence. It's a kind of ego-transcendence where the only thing that matters is what you're doing, not how you look while doing it.

4. *A sense of personal control or agency over the situation.* Flow doesn't mean the task is easy. In fact, in most cases, the task stretches you. But only a little. Enough to test your skills, but you still feel capable of meeting the challenge. There's a sense of mastery, where your skills are sufficient to deal with what's in front of you, even if it's demanding. In motorcycling, this is the balance point where you're not overwhelmed, nor are you bored, either – just fully in command of the ride.

5. *An altered experience of time (dilation or contraction).* When you're in flow, time becomes irrelevant. Time seems to either speed up or slow down dramatically. Hours can pass in what feels like minutes, or a few seconds seem to stretch out indefinitely, when you're highly focused. On a long solo ride, it's not unusual to "lose" an hour because your attention has been so fully absorbed in the act of riding.

6. *The activity is inherently rewarding.* You do the activity for its own sake, not for external rewards like money, praise or recognition. The process is the payoff. Motorcyclists often speak of riding as something that brings joy, clarity and satisfaction, because the act itself is fulfilling, not because of a destination or outcome. Flow is autotelic; it asks for no outcome beyond the moment. This is why riders speak of feeling most alive when riding nowhere in particular.

7. *Clear goals and immediate feedback.* Flow arises when you know what you're trying to achieve and can see, feel or sense whether you're succeeding. Whether it's carving a perfect corner, maintaining a smooth throttle through a windy section, or staying in rhythm with the road, you're constantly adjusting and improving in real time. This feedback loop sharpens focus and sustains momentum.

8. *A balance between challenge and skill.* Flow lives in the fertile ground between comfort and chaos. This is the central condition for entering flow. Too easy, and you'll fall asleep. Too hard, and fear and anxiety will take over. But when your skills and the task are fairly evenly matched – just enough to stretch you – you enter that sweet spot where growth, engagement and satisfaction converge.

Fear on the roads reduces the possibility of flow

Fear is something all riders experience at some point, but it hit differently on this particular Thursday in April 2025. Ian and I were making our way back to my place after a week of riding through Victoria, only to find ourselves caught in heavy traffic heading to the AFL Gather Round weekend in Adelaide. The freeway was packed with interstate travellers, and it felt like a pressure cooker. Half of Victoria seemed to be going the same way as us. Among the sea of cars, three P-plate drivers stood out. They were behaving erratically, speeding past us, tailgating whoever was in front of them, and clearly trying to outdo each other in their misbehaviour. The fear of being too close to them crept up as we rode. It was a testosterone-fuelled display of reckless driving, and it was scary. A disaster waiting to happen. After enduring their reckless antics for about fifteen kilometres, we decided to make an unscheduled stop, letting them get far ahead to reduce the danger of our being in their path.

When I face a dangerous situation on the road, such as the one described above or approaching a sharp bend too fast or dodging an unexpected obstacle on the road, I usually experience a tightening sensation in the chest or abdomen. This is a typical physical reaction to fear. As previously mentioned, somatic psychotherapies, for example, Bioenergetics and Radix, are based on the fundamental premise that there is a strong body-mind connection, that the body and mind are functionally identical; that is, what happens in the body is a direct reflection of the mind, and vice versa. This approach posits that the mind and body are not separate entities but, rather, interconnected systems that influence one another.

Research conducted by Stanford, UCLA and Washington University in St. Louis has significantly advanced our understanding of the intricate connection between fear, the brain and the body. Of particular relevance is research led by Washington University which discovered the somato-cognitive action network (SCAN), a brain network that links motor functions with cognitive processes, showing the connection between the brain and body in emotional responses such as fear. Further studies have elucidated how fear originates in the brain, manifests physically, and influences both mental and physical health.

Fear in the Warrumbungle Ranges

I remember a time when Ian and I had camped in the Warrumbungle Ranges northwest of Sydney. We had left in sunshine the next morning, but within an hour, the sun had disappeared, and we were caught in an unexpected torrential downpour. The sky had darkened, and fog was rolling in fast, making it a challenge to see the road ahead. It was scary. Not just mentally but physically, too. I was sweating and could feel tension around my shoulders and a tightness in my belly. My heart was beating faster. I was face-to-face with visceral fear and in danger of freezing because of it, so I had to take some deep breaths, move my body around the seat, and trust the bike and my riding experience. The extreme of this state lasted about ten minutes, but years later, I can still recall my physical reactions very clearly.

The traditional approach of conquering, suppressing or ignoring fear is misguided. Fear is a powerful, primal emotion that affects the body and mind in distinct ways. Various experts have explored the mechanisms of fear, its bodily effects, and how it shapes human behaviour. Treating fear as an adversary, something to be crushed in pursuit of greater feats, leads to burnout and mental exhaustion. Instead, we need to identify and acknowledge fear in our system, usually manifesting as a tightness in our body.

Flow Psychology: When the Rider and Machine Become One

It's not just in motorcycling ... Laird Hamilton, fear and flow

In a sport based on pushing the limits of surfing, legendary big-wave surfer Laird Hamilton is perhaps the one who has pushed the limits the most. Hamilton views fear as a powerful emotion that, when harnessed, can be a source of strength and heightened awareness rather than a paralysing force. His courageous approach to surfing has turned him into a well-respected global icon and source of inspiration for many. According to Hamilton, the best preparation for facing fear is to practise regular risk-taking. Then, "Once you start confronting your fears, you quickly realise that imagination is greater than reality, the thing is not so scary."

Why motorcyclists fear SMIDSYs

Every experienced motorcyclist knows the term "SMIDSY" all too well. It stands for "Sorry mate, I didn't see you" – a phrase often used by car drivers after they've either hit a rider or caused a near-miss that has sent them off their bike. It is a grim reality that motorcyclists are small, vulnerable objects on the road, and far too often, drivers simply don't see us. The thought of being struck by another vehicle is a genuine fear for riders. It's not just terrifying; it's painful. I've had my share of spills, but, thankfully, I've never been hit by another vehicle, and I plan to keep it that way. In fact, I can't think of anything that would rip me out of a flow state quicker than being hit by a car.

Over the years, I've taught around a dozen people how to drive or ride. As part of their training, I always encouraged drivers to shout "BIKE!" every time they saw a motorcyclist. It's a small action, but it drastically improves awareness. However, motorcyclists also have a responsibility. We need to avoid riding in another vehicle's blind spot, and we must focus on the road at least two to three cars ahead of us. By anticipating what's coming up, we give ourselves precious seconds to react and avoid potential danger.

When fear is acknowledged and accepted, it integrates into the flow state rather than disrupting it.

Fear can also be a learned response, where just thinking about potential dangers triggers the body's stress responses. When a rider is out in a challenging or unfamiliar environment, for example, navigating through dense fog or riding on a slippery wet road, their brain may perceive those conditions as threats. Even with my many years of experience, I still often react as if in danger. I feel my heart rate increase and my muscles tighten up as my amygdala signals for the release of adrenaline. This process heightens my sense of alertness, but it also makes it necessary for me to consciously breathe and regulate my emotional state.

Why flow matters

Experiencing flow transforms ordinary tasks into enjoyable experiences and elevates high-achievement moments into deeply meaningful ones. Flow is more than simply reaching peak performance. It creates a state of mind that leads to satisfaction, productivity and happiness. By understanding and nurturing flow, we open ourselves up to a world of endless possibilities.

Clarity of purpose plays a pivotal role in achieving flow. When it is combined with curiosity and passion, the chances of entering the flow state increase dramatically. To experience flow regularly, focus on developing these traits. Passion gives the task more meaning. Curiosity drives the desire to explore, discover and push beyond your current limits.

When it comes to setting goals, it's crucial that the level of challenge matches your capabilities. To attain flow, the goal should push you marginally beyond your comfort zone but remain achievable. This creates the sweet spot where flow can thrive. The more you engage with this challenge through practice and training, the more you grow. With each step, your skills develop and your confidence strengthens. This growth boosts your self-esteem and allows you to raise the bar for future goals. You'll notice that your

Flow Psychology: When the Rider and Machine Become One

goals expand as your abilities solidify, and what was once a stretch will become your new baseline.

While the experience of flow can sometimes feel like magic, when the stars align and everything simply clicks, there are also ways to intentionally create the conditions for it. Flow often emerges when all the elements align, but mindfulness plays a role in guiding us towards those moments. By breaking through what you previously thought was possible and striving for higher goals, you unlock the focus, motivation, and productivity needed to achieve even your most ambitious dreams.

This idea was expressed by American philosopher and psychologist William James in "The Energies of Man", delivered as the presidential address to the American Theosophical Society at Columbia University on 6 December 6 1906:

The human individual thus lives usually far within his limits; he possesses powers of various sorts which he habitually fails to use. He energizes below his maximum, and he behaves below his optimum ... in every conceivable way, his life is contracted like the field of vision of a hysteric subject – but with less excuse, for the poor hysteric is diseased, while in the rest of us, it is only an inveterate habit – the habit of inferiority to our full self – that is bad.

James's message was clear: many of us don't live up to our full potential, not because we can't, but because we've never learned the habit of doing so. The habit of living below our potential is the real "disease" of human behaviour. By setting clear stretch goals, ones that push you 10 to 20 percent beyond your current limits, you can begin to change this pattern and tap into flow more frequently.

As touring motorcyclists, Ian and I have experienced flow countless times, and I know I'm not alone. Many riders, especially those on long-distance journeys, report entering a state of flow, particularly on open roads that allow for smooth, rhythmic riding. The repetitive motions of such riding can create a meditative state in which focus is natural and distractions fade away.

The Open Road Within

Recently, I came across a post on a motorcycle forum by a solo rider named Paul, who shared his experience of flow. Paul's reflection on his ride through the Canadian Rockies captures beautifully the essence of flow in motorcycling:

Somewhere between the fifth and sixth hour of riding through the Canadian Rockies, I realised I hadn't really thought about anything for miles. No stress, no work, no problems – just riding. Every gear shift, every curve, every roll of the throttle felt completely automatic, yet fully conscious at the same time. I wasn't separate from the bike; I was in the ride. That's why I keep coming back to motorcycling – it's the only time my mind feels this clear.

Paul's experience highlights how long-distance riding can induce flow by allowing the rider to enter a rhythm of continuous motion, often accompanied by solitude and immersion in the ride. This sense of oneness with the bike, where the mind is calm and the body moves almost instinctively, is a hallmark of flow for many touring motorcyclists.

Incorporating flow into our lives – whether on the bike, in the workplace or at home – offers powerful benefits. It helps us tap into our potential and feel deeply engaged with what we do. Therefore, achieving flow not only helps us to improve our performance but it also enhances our experience of life itself, turning every task into opportunities to grow, learn and enjoy the ride.

Chapter 6:

RESPONSIBILITY

Simon and Lisa's story: A lesson in responsibility

In 2020, the famous adventure motorcycling duo of *2RideTheWorld*, Simon and Lisa Thomas, came to the end of a seventeen-year, 500,000-mile round-the-world odyssey through eighty countries. Taking responsibility and being incredibly resilient and resourceful were everyday realities for this adventurous couple.

Their journey included riding Siberia's notorious Kolyma Highway (the "Road of Bones"), crossing the Sahara Desert and navigating war zones in Africa. They kept going despite serious mechanical issues, a near-fatal food poisoning incident in the Amazon, and many other extreme challenges. In 2017 they experienced their most serious test when Simon had a near-fatal accident in the US. While riding off-road, he misjudged a water crossing, hit an unseen rock, and was thrown violently forward. His injuries included a broken neck, a shattered shoulder and severe internal damage. After a hospital stay and a recuperation period for Simon, the couple kept going and finished what became one of the most epic motorcycle journeys ever documented.

It would have been easy to give up after the accident. Many would have looked for reasons and excuses to stop. Instead, Simon took full responsibility, acknowledging his fatigue and the poor choices he had made leading up to the accident. After the incident, he shifted his focus towards helping others by sharing his lessons on risk management, personal responsibility and resilience.

Simon's and Lisa's story is a powerful example of how you can turn a negative experience into a catalyst for positive change. Not only did they take responsibility, but they also saw it as an opportunity for growth rather than simply blaming external conditions. They remain involved in the adventure riding community, giving inspirational talks, writing articles and coaching riders on safety, resilience and round-the-world travel.

Simon and Lisa are the living embodiments of the three R's: responsibility, resilience and resourcefulness, which will be covered in the next two chapters. Their experience is a clear example of the theme of this chapter. It's not what happens to you that matters; the important thing is how you respond.

Taking responsibility is a choice

Just as a rider chooses their line through a corner, we choose ours through life's challenges. In that choice lies a subtle but profound truth: we are not merely passengers on the road of life; we are active participants who are shaping our journeys. Responsibility, at its core, is an act of creative authorship, a declaration that "I will navigate this bend, however tight, with intention and courage." Every challenge, every setback, is like a curve in the road. It demands awareness, commitment and trust in ourselves. By choosing the line we will take, rather than letting the road dictate our path. We engage with life as a co-creator, not a passive observer.

I wasn't supposed to see Christmas 2022

It was mid-January 2022. Miranda and I and our teenagers were on holiday at a beach just south of Adelaide. I remember it was a hot day. The phone rang just as I was getting out of the pool. It was my skin specialist, and it wasn't good news.

A week before, I had gone to see the specialist about a lesion on my scalp. (I am basically bald.) He didn't like the look of it, so he biopsied it and sent the sample to the lab. The call was to tell me it was a melanoma. I made an appointment to see him at the Royal Adelaide Hospital in a few days. By the time of the appointment, several other lesions had appeared. Things were not looking good.

I met with my dermatologist, who immediately made a couple of phone calls. In minutes, I was in front of the chief of radiology, and within half an hour after that, I met with the professor in charge of the cancer unit who, thankfully, had agreed to see me at such short notice. Things were moving quickly, and they were looking worse by the minute. It was made clear to me that I'd be lucky to see Christmas and that treatment was optional. I opted for immunotherapy to treat what had now been diagnosed as "multiple serious melanomas".

I knew I had a rocky road in front of me. This was a whole new world for Miranda and me. The treatment path was going to test not only my body but also my mindset. Whatever the outcome, I knew I had to take responsibility for the treatment journey that I was embarking on. I knew I had to control my mindset (especially Crocky) and control what I focused on. It would have been easy to dive into a victim mentality and ask endless looped questions: *Why me? Why this? Why now?* But I knew that would only make things worse. So, I did everything I could think of that was in my control. I changed my diet, increased my exercise, started meditating again, and did a lot of creative visualisations that focused on my ridding myself of melanoma.

I knew I had choices. I used to say to coaching clients that when you have a tiger in your life, it's up to you if you lie down and let the tiger eat you – or not. Now I took my own advice. I wasn't going to let this tiger eat me without a fight! This is what I mean by taking responsibility. I couldn't control the melanoma, but I could control how I thought about it and my general mindset and behaviour.

Initially, I received several heavy doses of radiotherapy, and this was followed by several doses of immunotherapy. It worked miracles. Before the Christmas I wasn't supposed to see, my head was totally clear of any melanomas! I have had the all-clear at all my six-monthly scans since then, and things are looking good.

This experience taught me that responsibility isn't just doing what you're told by the doctors or following a treatment plan. You have to own every part of the journey: your mindset, your actions and even your attitude. When I felt like giving in to fear or self-pity, I reminded myself that while I couldn't control the cancer, I *could* control how I approached it. I chose to face each appointment, each scan and each sleepless night with as much courage and positivity as I could muster. That experience reinforced to me that responsibility means stepping up to life's challenges, no matter how big they seem, and taking ownership of how you respond to them.

Personal Responsibility – The Author's Road

Responsibility Is the Turning Point

Taking responsibility is the moment you stop drifting and start living. It means owning your choices, your reactions, and even the parts of yourself you'd rather pretend don't exist. It's uncomfortable work, digging into the darker corners of your personality, admitting mistakes, or facing how much of your suffering is self-inflicted. But without it, growth stalls.

"Responsibility is not a burden; it is the key to growth."

Responsibility Is Not Blame

Many people hear the word "responsibility" and immediately think of fault, guilt, or punishment. But responsibility is not blame. It's not about beating yourself up or carrying the failures of others. Responsibility means ownership. While you cannot control everything that happens, you can always control how you respond. That is where real power lives. In choosing your response, you stop being a passive actor in someone else's play and instead become the author of your own story.

Actor or author? The choice is yours.

Why People Resist Responsibility

If responsibility is so empowering, why do people avoid it? Heree's a few reasons:

- Excuses and blame offer an easy escape from the hard truth that you are both the problem and the solution.

- Shame makes us fear that admitting responsibility will expose us as "not enough." As Brené Brown points out, shame drives us to armour up with denial or deflection.

- Biology works against us too. Robert Sapolsky in his book, Behave, shows how hormones and stress hijack the brain, narrowing perspective and pushing us into defensive behaviours before we even think. Old conditioning often runs the show.

Avoidance isn't always laziness, it's often self-protection. But protection comes at the cost of growth.

Responsibility as an Existential Stance

Responsibility is not just a rational decision; it's an existential stance. Psychiatrist Viktor Frankl, who survived the concentration camps, captured it best:

> *"Between stimulus and response, there is a space. In that space is our power to choose our response. In our response lies our growth and our freedom."*

Responsibility is that space. It's the recognition that you are not defined by events, but by the meaning you give them and the actions you take. Like a motorcyclist confronted with an unexpected obstacle, you can either panic and freeze or respond with skill and presence. The obstacle remains, but your response defines the outcome.

A Word on the Shadow

Carl Jung pointed out that much of what we avoid is not the world, but ourselves. He described the "shadow" as the traits we bury, selfishness, anger, arrogance, because they feel unacceptable. But what we deny doesn't disappear; it shows up as projection. We accuse others of being what we secretly fear in ourselves. (There's more about the shadow in a future chapter).

Taking responsibility means reclaiming those projections. Saying, *"Yes, selfishness is in me. Anger is in me. And I am responsible for how I live with that."* This is difficult and sometimes confronting work, but freeing. When you stop projecting, you stop fighting shadows outside yourself and begin shaping life from within.

The Stoic Road

The Stoics were blunt. Marcus Aurelius wrote: *"You have power over your mind, not outside events. Realise this, and you will find strength."* Epictetus taught that freedom comes from recognising what is "up to you" and what is not. On the road, this is obvious: you cannot control rain, wind, or potholes. But you can control your preparation, your choices, and your mindset.

Complaining about the weather won't dry the road. Slowing down, leaning carefully, and adjusting your riding will get you through. That is the Stoic essence of responsibility.

Motorcycling and Responsibility

On a motorcycle, responsibility is immediate and unavoidable. Every action has consequences. The bike listens only to you. Lean too late, brake too hard, or drift off line, and you pay the price.

But responsibility is also what makes riding exhilarating. The very fact that your choices matter so much is what makes you feel alive.

Life is no different. You can't control everything thrown at you. But you can control how you ride it—whether you lean in with presence or hand over control to fear and blame.

On the bike, as in life, you are the rider. No one else can lean for you.

Why Responsibility Matters

Refusing responsibility leads to victimhood and powerlessness. Life becomes something that "happens to you." But taking responsibility restores agency. You accept ownership for your actions and reactions, your decisions and their consequences, without taking on what is not yours.

For me, personal responsibility means being the author of my own life, not a passive character in someone else's story. I am responsible for my evolution, my choices, and the meaning I create. That responsibility is both sobering and liberating.

In the end, responsibility is the paradox of freedom. By letting go of the illusion of control over the world, you gain real power over yourself. By choosing authorship instead of victimhood, you discover that the road, whatever its twists and detours, can be your road, your story, your ride.

Understanding why people avoid taking responsibility can help us gain deeper insights into human behaviour and develop more effective strategies for fostering self-awareness and empowerment. Here are a few more common reasons:

1. Fear of failure

Several years ago, I was on a three-week tour of New Zealand's North Island, an incredible place for motorcycling. I'd spent weeks planning the trip, making sure my bike, gear and route were all in order. Yet as I navigated the winding roads of the Coromandel Peninsula, doubts crept in. Was I truly prepared? Did I have the skill for the tight, technical corners ahead?

One particular hairpin bend stands out in my memory. As I leaned into it, my bike suddenly slid on a mix of oil and loose gravel. I froze. It was just for a split second, but it was enough to feel real fear. I'd faced far more dangerous situations, but at that moment, the fear of failure took over. What if I couldn't handle it? What if I lost control?

I managed to regain control of the bike, but the experience stayed with me. I realised how the fear of failure can paralyse us and distort our judgement. I had been going too fast in that bend, and deep down, I knew it. It would have been easier to blame external factors, but I took responsibility and accepted the blame.

That ride taught me that failure itself doesn't define me. But how I respond to it does. The next time I faced a similar bend, I took a deep breath, recalled my training, and rode through with calm focus. That shift in mindset helped me accept responsibility for my actions and trust my own skills.

2. External locus of control

In 2023, Ian and I rode to Western Australia. At the beginning of the Nullarbor, we met a Harley rider named John who asked if we were okay with him riding along with us. John had been riding for over twenty years, but, despite his experience, he complained often about the challenges he faced on the road. He'd say, "The weather's against us," or "The roads are too dangerous today." He'd blame everything around him. It was always the wind's, the traffic's or the terrain's fault. He rarely considered that his own actions might be contributing to his difficulties.

One afternoon, as we approached a particularly tricky section of roadworks in strong winds, John pulled over, frustrated with the conditions, while we continued on. When I checked in after he'd caught up, he told me he couldn't ride safely in those conditions. "It's just too dangerous out there." It was then that I realised that John was failing to take responsibility for his own decisions. The wind was certainly strong, but that wasn't an excuse for not riding at a pace that suited his skill level. He had an external "locus of control"; thus, he attributed his difficulties to everything outside his control, rather than adjusting his speed and discipling his self-talk.

It was a reminder that we have more control over our actions than we sometimes acknowledge. By taking responsibility for our choices, we can often find ways to adapt and improve, rather than being at the mercy of circumstances. John's story shows how an external locus of control can feed into a victim mindset.

3. The comfort of victimhood

I was riding through a small town in New South Wales when I came across a rider who had been stranded by a mechanical failure. His bike had broken down in the middle of nowhere, and he was visibly frustrated. He had been waiting for hours for roadside assistance. When I stopped to offer help, he explained that this had been the third time in a month that his bike had broken down. "I can't catch a break," he said. "Everything's going wrong in my life right now."

As I listened to him, it became clear that he had adopted a victim mentality. Instead of taking responsibility for his bike's maintenance or addressing any of the underlying issues with his riding habits, he had resigned himself to the belief that life was simply working against him. The bike breaking down was just another instance of bad luck in a string of misfortunes.

I suggested to him that he might benefit from taking a more proactive approach, for example, regularly servicing his bike, investing in preventative maintenance, and even learning some basic troubleshooting skills. In essence, I was suggesting that he prepare for challenges and take responsibility for the things within his control. After a lengthy discussion, he began to see that he could shift his mindset and take more ownership of his circumstances.

Adopting a victim mentality may be comforting in the short term, as it absolves you of responsibility. But in the long run, it keeps you stuck in a cycle of helplessness. True growth and empowerment come when we accept responsibility for our actions, whether it's maintaining our bikes or confronting the difficulties in our lives head on.

The consequences of avoiding responsibility

Avoiding responsibility leads to stagnation, frustration and continually being a victim of circumstances and other people. When we blame circumstances or others, we give away our power. Over time, this mindset will lead to chronic dissatisfaction, feeling stuck and repeating the same mistakes without learning from them. It will also strain relationships. Blaming others for our personal failures erodes trust and respect in both personal and professional settings. Moreover, people who avoid responsibility also tend to struggle with self-esteem, feeling helpless and lacking confidence in their ability to effect change.

Neuroscience has shown that a lack of perceived control increases our levels of cortisol, the body's primary stress hormone. Elevated cortisol leads to heightened stress and anxiety, which in turn affect mental and physical health.

The science of responsibility

As stated above, research has consistently shown the benefits of taking personal responsibility. People with an internal locus of control, that is, those who believe they can influence their own lives, report greater motivation, achievement, and well-being.

When we focus on what lies outside our control, we set ourselves up for frustration. At best, it leads to disappointment, at worst, to feelings of powerlessness and even neurosis. The model below, the Wheel of Control, illustrates this idea using three concentric circles, with the hub of the wheel representing what we can directly control.

Responsibility

THE WHEEL OF CONTROL

FREEDOM IS FOCUSING ON WHAT YOU CAN SHAPE, NOT WHAT YOU CAN'T.

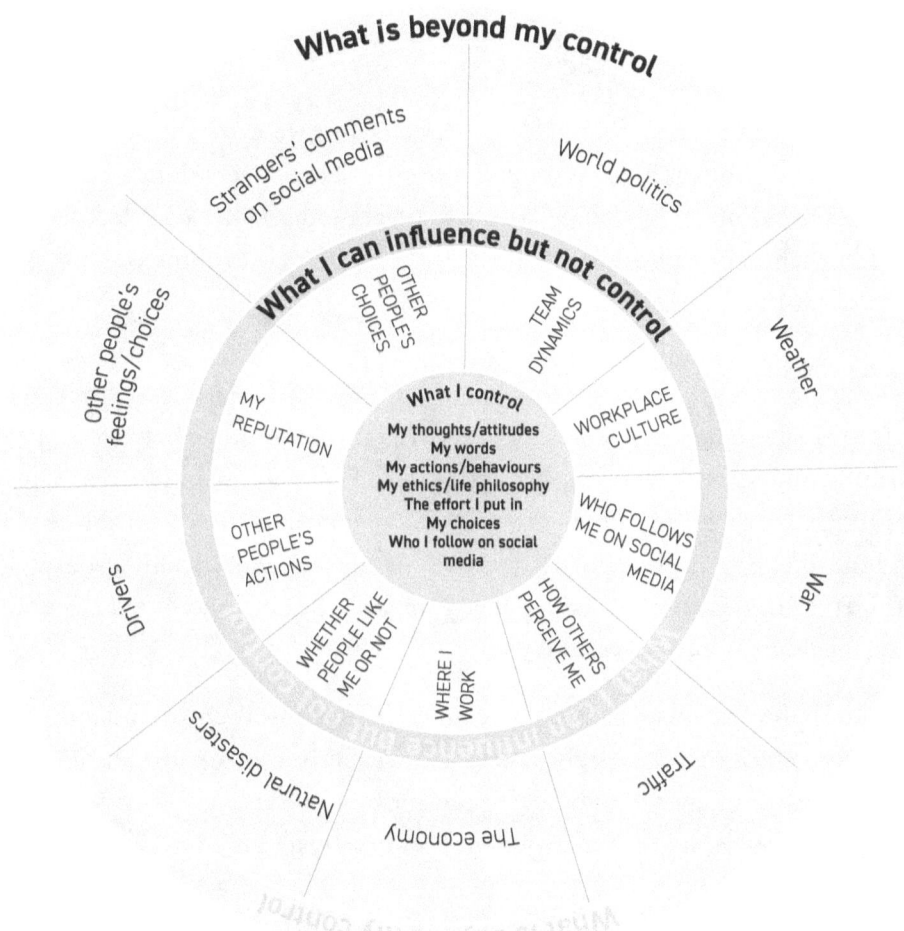

The Circle of Concern (Outer Ring):

This includes things we may worry about but over which we have little or no control. Obsessing over these leads to frustration and helplessness. If you pour your energy into solving global issues such as war, world peace, childhood hunger, or climate change, or into fretting over what strangers say about you on social media, you'll almost certainly end up disheartened.

The Circle of Influence (Middle Ring):

Here, we cannot control outcomes directly, but we can make an impact through our choices, behaviour, and attitudes. This covers things such as workplace culture, who follows you on social media, other people's decisions, or whether or not others like you. You don't control the outcome, but your influence matters.

The Circle of Control (The Hub of the Wheel):

This is where real power lies: in your thoughts, emotions, behaviour, philosophy of life, and even who you choose to follow on social media. These are things no one else can take from you. By focusing energy on the Hub and the Circle of Influence, we cultivate stability, resilience, and a sense of agency. In contrast, investing energy in what lies beyond our reach will leave us drained and powerless.

When circumstances cannot be changed, resisting them is futile. But in every situation, two things always remain within our grasp: our attitude and how we run our lives day by day. Shifting how we think and respond can completely reshape how we experience and navigate life's challenges.

I've found that the best attitude is one that makes the best use of what is in your power and takes the rest as it happens. Some things are up to us, and some things are not. Our opinions are up to us, as are our impulses, desires, and aversions – in short, whatever is our own doing.

Research indicates that the prefrontal cortex, the part of the brain responsible for decision-making and self-regulation, is more active in individuals who take ownership of their actions. Conversely, those who frequently blame external factors exhibit greater activity in the amygdala, the brain's fear and stress centre, leading to increased anxiety and defensiveness.

Traits and habits of responsible people

People who embrace responsibility tend to display key traits and habits that contribute to both their personal and professional success. More than just following through with tasks, a responsible person also embodies a mindset that fosters growth, resilience and integrity. Below are the foundational qualities that make such individuals stand out, with motorcycling examples to bring these traits to life.

Self-awareness

Responsible individuals consistently practise self-awareness by actively developing their inner witness. They take time to reflect on their actions, emotions and decisions, recognising how they impact both themselves and others. This introspection allows them to identify areas for growth and develop a deeper understanding of their strengths and weaknesses. Being self-aware is essential for making informed choices and remaining grounded in the face of life's challenges.

For example, on a long ride, a rider might notice they're becoming fatigued or tense and that it is affecting their performance. By recognising these signs early, they can pull over to take a break, practice deep breathing or assess their riding posture, making sure they stay focused and safe on the road. This self-awareness helps them avoid accidents and keeps them in control, thus doing what they can to contribute to their safety and well-being throughout the journey.

A possibility mindset

A mindset focused on possibilities rather than obstacles is crucial for responsible individuals. They believe that their abilities and intelligence can be developed through dedication and hard work. Rather than seeing challenges as obstacles, they view them as opportunities to learn, evolve and improve.

This mindset fuels their continuous improvement and empowers them to embrace change and adversity with confidence.

Perhaps a rider struggles to navigate tight curves at higher speeds. Instead of seeing this as an impossible skill to master, they might attend a training course. Through practice and persistence, they will gradually become more confident in handling curves, thus turning what had initially seemed insurmountable into an area of personal growth.

Integrity

Integrity is the foundation of responsibility. People who exhibit integrity consistently align their actions with their values and principles. They do what they say they will do and hold themselves accountable for their commitments. This trait builds trust with others and reinforces their sense of personal responsibility. Integrity leads them to make ethical decisions, even when no one is watching.

The responsible motorcyclist commits to maintaining their bike regularly to ensure that it's safe for long rides. Despite the temptation to delay maintenance to save time or money, they keep their promise to themselves to prioritise the bike's upkeep. By doing so, they contribute to their safety and that of others on the road, thus demonstrating integrity in their actions.

Resilience

Resilience, the second of the three R's (responsibility, resilience and resourcefulness), is the ability to bounce back from setbacks. Responsible individuals don't dwell on their mistakes or failures; instead, they take lessons from them to grow stronger. They possess the emotional fortitude to face difficulties head on, remain adaptable in the face of adversity, and continue moving forward with determination.

After an unexpected low-speed spill on a wet road in Port Fairy, Victoria, I had to work to control my thoughts, because I was in danger of letting this incident define my abilities as a motorcyclist. Instead of feeling discouraged by this minor incident or giving up riding, I took time to analyse what had gone wrong, and I got feedback from Ian, who had witnessed the incident. As a result, I returned to the road with renewed confidence. There was no one else to blame for me coming off the bike. Resilience allowed me to learn from the experience and, thus, use it as a stepping stone to future growth.

Initiative

Initiative is a habit that propels responsible individuals into action. They do not wait for circumstances to improve or for others to take charge. Instead, they take the lead. Showing initiative demonstrates commitment to making things happen and taking ownership of circumstances, rather than waiting for external forces to dictate the pace of change.

A motorcyclist on a group ride notices that one of the riders is struggling to keep up due to a mechanical issue. Instead of waiting for someone else to step in, they take the initiative to pull over with the other rider to offer them help. They help to troubleshoot the issue and get the rider back on the road and into the group, thereby showing leadership and a proactive approach to ensuring the group's success.

Accountability

Responsible individuals don't shy away from acknowledging their mistakes. They are willing to take full accountability for their actions and decisions, without blaming external factors or other people. This transparency builds credibility and demonstrates their commitment to personal and professional growth. Accountability also extends to others; responsible people hold others to their word while at the same time providing them support and encouragement.

After completing a long tour, a rider reflects on their trip and realises that they had missed a few key waypoints due to poor planning. Instead of blaming unforeseen circumstances, they take full responsibility for not having researched the route more thoroughly. This accountability leads them to adjust their planning process for future trips. They'll be better prepared next time.

Time management

Effective time management is a key habit of responsible individuals. They prioritise tasks, set clear goals, and follow through on deadlines. They recognise that both short-term responsibilities and long-term objectives are important. By managing their time well, they avoid the "need" for procrastination and stay on track even when faced with competing demands.

A rider planning a cross-country trip factors in regular rest stops, overnight accommodations, and time to explore local sights. They set realistic daily travel goals, knowing that balancing time on the bike with proper rest and leisure will lead to a safer and more enjoyable journey.

Emotional regulation

Responsible people are skilled at regulating their emotions, especially in high-stress situations. They remain calm and composed even when things don't go as planned. This emotional control enables them to think critically and make rational decisions under pressure. By practicing emotional regulation, they avoid impulsive reactions and can instead choose responses that align with their values and goals.

While navigating through heavy traffic, a motorcyclist feels their stress level rising as vehicles crowd around them. Instead of succumbing to road rage or reacting impulsively in another way, they take a deep breath to calm themselves and focus on maintaining a safe distance. Emotional regulation keeps them safe and helps them to make responsible decisions while riding.

Empathy and compassion

Empathy is a key trait in a responsible individual. They consider the feelings, needs and perspectives of others, which fosters collaboration, trust and mutual respect. Whether in personal or professional relationships, they are supportive and compassionate, helping others when needed and remaining mindful of their emotional and mental well-being

When I was on a group ride with the Ulysses Club, one of the riders became anxious in rapidly changing weather conditions as an unexpected storm approached. I watched as a responsible rider noticed their discomfort and went to check that they were doing okay, offering words of encouragement and suggesting they take a break or adjust their speed. Their empathy helped the rider to feel supported and less isolated in their experience.

Resourcefulness

The ability to think creatively and find solutions is a hallmark of responsibility. Resourceful individuals don't wait for the perfect circumstances; they make the best of what they have, seeking out innovative solutions even when faced with limited resources. Their adaptability and problem-solving skills allow them to navigate complex situations with ease.

Be like Fred

I met a guy named Fred at Quorn at the edge of the Flinders Ranges. Fred was doing the big lap (this is what Australian motorcyclists call riding around Australia) on a Suzuki DR650 and told me about his adventures over a beer in the local pub. He'd been riding solo along the Oodnadatta Track in outback South Australia, hundreds of kilometres from the nearest mechanic. Suddenly, his clutch cable snapped, leaving him stranded in the middle of nowhere. No spare cable, no phone signal, no roadside assist and very little, if any, passing traffic.

Luckily, he lived on a farm, so he was accustomed to improvising. Instead of panicking, he dug through his kit and spotted a roll of wire he'd thrown into his bag as a last-minute addition. With a bit of ingenuity, he twisted the wire into a makeshift cable, threaded it through the lever and clutch arm, and secured it tight with pliers from his tool roll. It was rough, stiff, and far from perfect, but it got him to Coober Pedy, where he stayed four nights waiting for a cable to be brought over 800 kilometres by courier from Adelaide. Needless to say, he bought two cables just in case it happened again.

That's resourcefulness on two wheels: taking what you've got, thinking laterally, and refusing to let a setback end the ride.

In a nutshell ....

By learning, practising and embodying these traits and habits, an individual can cultivate a sense of personal responsibility that fosters growth, success and resilience in every aspect of their life – whether on the motorcycle or beyond.

The impact of responsibility in daily life

Responsibility plays a vital role in many aspects of life, influencing how we interact with others, manage our well-being, and pursue personal growth.

In the workplace, individuals who embrace responsibility tend to excel in leadership and problem-solving. Their proactivity earns them trust and respect. Similarly, in relationships, taking ownership of one's role in conflicts fosters stronger, more open connections, whereas blaming others erodes trust. Responsibility in health and well-being looks like making better decisions about diet, exercise and stress management. Financial stability often grows out of taking responsibility for spending, saving and investing wisely. Those who embrace responsibility actively seek self-improvement because it leads to greater fulfilment and success.

Consider a team leader facing a project that has fallen behind schedule. They could blame team members, unclear instructions or external delays. However, a responsible leader would take a step back and ask, "What could I have done differently? Did I set clear expectations? Did I provide the necessary resources and guidance?" This mindset allows the leader to adjust their approach and prevent future setbacks.

Responsibility

A common misconception about personal responsibility is that it equals self-blame or assigning blame to others. In truth and to reinforce what I have already stated, responsibility is about acknowledging reality, including acknowledging one's faults as a starting point for doing something different next time. For example, if a motorcyclist were to get caught in the rain without proper gear, they could blame the weather, the forecaster or bad luck. Alternatively, they could reflect on their oversight in not checking the forecast and commit to packing rain gear in the future. This simple approach leads to growth and better outcomes.

Examples in the workplace, family, and riding

In family dynamics, a parent who frequently argues with their teenager might blame their child's attitude or defiance. A responsible parent, however, might reflect on their communication style and ask, "Am I truly listening? Am I setting consistent boundaries and encouraging a respectful environment?"

A motorcyclist cut off by a car might instinctively blame the driver. But a responsible rider will ask, "Did I anticipate this situation? Was I in their blind spot? Could I have adjusted my positioning for better safety? Was I watching two or three cars ahead?" While this doesn't excuse poor driving, cultivating an attitude like this will empower the rider to take proactive steps to improve their safety.

The story of Jim Stockdale: Responsibility to endure

Jim Stockdale, a US Navy pilot shot down during the Vietnam War, endured over seven years of captivity, surviving torture and solitary confinement. Despite his harrowing circumstances, Stockdale took full responsibility for enduring his captivity and for his duty to lead and protect his fellow prisoners.

Stockdale's approach formed the basis of what author Jim Collins coined the Stockdale Paradox. In his book *Good to Great*, Collins quotes the advice that Stockdale gave him: "You must never confuse faith that you will prevail in the end – which you can never afford to lose – with the discipline to confront the most brutal facts of your current reality, whatever they might be." Even though he was physically tortured no fewer than fifteen times, instead of blaming his captors or the situation, Stockdale took charge of his mindset and actions. He found ways to resist, for example, communicating with the other prisoners by tapping codes, and he refused to let his captors break his spirit. His story teaches that responsibility involves choosing how we respond to adversity, taking ownership of our attitudes and actions, and accepting what we cannot change. During his stay at the "Hanoi Hilton" that lasted from 1965 to 1973, Stockdale did not lose faith that he would prevail in the end.

Beware the Valley of Reasons and Excuses

Success is not an accident. It is the direct result of taking responsibility and holding yourself accountable for doing what needs to be done, without giving excuses or reasons for your failures. Happiness and success don't simply happen to lucky people. They happen to those who step up, take control and own their actions.

However, many people choose to live in what I call the Valley of Reasons and Excuses. They always have a story to tell – a story that, at first glance, may sound convincing, but when you strip away the drama, the justifications and the debate, the core message remains the same:

"It's not my fault."

They point to circumstances, external forces, people and past events as the reasons they aren't where they want to be. They list the obstacles as if the presence of such hurdles has absolved them from acting. But if you look deeper, you'll find one simple truth: they didn't take responsibility for doing what needed to be done.

In life, you have two choices:

Take responsibility and do your utmost to create the outcomes you desire; or be a victim and make excuses and create reasons that will keep you stuck.

It really is that simple.

At the end of the day, reasons and excuses don't matter. The world doesn't slow down to accommodate them. Circumstances will never be perfect, and waiting for them to become perfect is just another excuse in disguise.

This truth is nothing new. In George Bernard Shaw's 1893 play *Mrs. Warren's Profession*, the character Vivie puts it plainly: "People are always blaming their circumstances for what they are. I don't believe in circumstances. The people who get on in this world are the people who get up and look for the circumstances they want, and, if they can't find them, make them."

So, the question is: Are you choosing reasons and excuses, or are you choosing to take responsibility for your results?

Because in the end, the choice is always yours.

Choosing responsibility, choosing freedom

The line we choose on the road and in life is ours alone. Responsibility isn't about controlling everything that happens to us. It's about controlling how we respond and how we grow from every twist and turn. The choice is always ours: either blame the road or own your ride. Every time you choose responsibility, you claim your power to shape your life. One decision, one curve, one day at a time. So, as you ride on, ask yourself: *What line will I choose today? Where in my life am I giving away responsibility? Where can I take it back?* Because, in the end, the road doesn't define you. What defines you is the line you choose to take. Whether on a bike or in life, the line we choose shapes both our journey and who we become. Responsibility is the art of choosing that line mindfully and shaping our path one bend at a time.

Personal responsibility is summed up beautifully in the following poem written by the American singer, songwriter, actress and author Portia Nelson.

The Open Road Within

Autobiography in Five Short Chapters

I.

I walk down the street; there is a deep hole in the sidewalk.

I fall in. I am lost. I am hopeless.

It isn't my fault.

It takes forever to find a way out.

II.

I walk down the street; there is a deep hole in the sidewalk.

I pretend I don't see it.   I fall in again.

I can't believe I'm in the same place.

But it isn't my fault.

It still takes a long time to get out.

III.

I walk down the same street.

There is a deep hole in the sidewalk.

I see it is there.   I still fall in.

It's a habit,

My eyes are open,

I know where I am.

It is my fault.

I get out immediately.

IV.

I walk down the same street.

There is a deep hole in the sidewalk.

I walk around it.

V.

I walk down another street.

Chapter 7:

RESILIENCE AND RESOURCEFULNESS

In many ways, life is just like motorcycling. It's full of twists, turns, unexpected bumps in the road, and the occasional flat tyre. Every rider knows that staying upright is more than just skill; it's also a mindset. Staying upright involves having the confidence to keep going when the road gets rough and having the creativity to find a way forward when the plan goes sideways. In other words, it requires resilience and resourcefulness, two qualities that everybody needs to thrive on the open road of life.

In Buddhist philosophy, *anicca* (impermanence) reminds us that everything is in constant flux. This understanding strengthens resilience by dissolving the illusion of control and inviting us to move with the natural cycles of change. Like a rider flowing through corners, we find steadiness by embracing movement – by going with the flow, not resisting it.

Think of resilience as the suspension that soaks up the bumps and keeps you steady, and resourcefulness as the map and toolkit that help you navigate and fix the inevitable detours. One keeps you grounded; the other keeps you moving. Let's explore how these two qualities intertwine and how they can help you stay upright both on the road and in life.

Resilience: The strength to keep going

On 19 July 1971, W. Mitchell experienced a life-altering motorcycle accident. His state-of-the-art Honda 750/4 motorcycle crashed into a laundry truck, and the fuel tank ignited. He suffered severe burns to most of his body, including his face, and he lost his fingers.

Life had more tests in store for Mitchell.

Four years later, he was in a plane crash that left him paralysed from the waist down. Despite this, he refused to see himself as a victim. Instead, he rebuilt his life, becoming a motivational speaker and best-selling author, advocating for personal responsibility and positive thinking. His mantra, also the title of his second book, is simple: "It's not what happens to you, it's what you do about it."

That's resilience!

Resilience is the ability to withstand adversity, adapt to challenges, and keep going despite setbacks. It's not avoiding difficulties and problems. That's impossible – and nor should you want to do that. As M. Scott Peck wrote in *The Road Less Travelled*, "It is in the process of meeting and solving problems that life has its meaning." Resilience is developing the self-assurance and inner strength to navigate problems and emerge stronger. In motorcycling, as in life, resilience is an essential trait. Every rider knows that the road isn't always smooth. There are unexpected detours, mechanical failures, kangaroos. Poor roads and tough weather conditions are part of the journey. The same is true in life, where personal and professional challenges test our ability to persevere.

Long-distance touring offers insight into resilience. More than once, I've set out on a ride in perfect conditions, only to encounter storms, a breakdown in the middle of nowhere, or injuring myself while off the bike. Some riders might see obstacles such as these as reasons to give up. Others, the resilient ones, will find ways to push forward by fixing the bike on the roadside, adjusting their route, or drawing on their mental reserves to keep moving. The ability to adapt and persist separates those who complete the journey from those who turn back.

Introducing CART: The resilience roadmap

On one particular ride, through the winding roads of Brown Mountain in southern NSW, I was alone on the bike, chasing a sunset that felt just out of reach. Suddenly, the road ahead disappeared in a blanket of fog. My first reaction was frustration: I had planned the ride meticulously, and the fog wasn't in my plan. Now, visibility was almost zero. But as I slowed down and adapted, I found a strange calm. I accepted the fog as part of the ride; something I couldn't control but could navigate. I committed to the ride, anyway, reframed the challenge as an opportunity to test my focus and skills, took extra care, and settled into a rhythm of riding suitable for the conditions. By the time I reached Bega, the fog had lifted, and I felt stronger for having faced it.

Resilience is a dynamic process, not a fixed trait. Over decades of riding and life coaching, I've developed the CART model: Commitment, Acceptance, Reframing, and Take Action. It's a personal roadmap to help navigate adversity.

The diagram that follows captures this roadmap visually, showing how each element feeds into the next. Just like the continuous flow of a winding road, the process of resilience is an ongoing cycle that strengthens with practice and experience.

CART - THE RESILIENCE ROADMAP

Now that you have a sense of how the CART model works as a whole, let's take a closer look at each step. By exploring each element individually – Commitment, Acceptance, Reframing, and Take Action – you'll see how they work together to build resilience to help you navigate life's curves.

- *Commitment* is about staying true to your values and purpose, no matter the terrain. On the bike, it's what keeps you moving forward despite fatigue or poor conditions.

- *Acceptance* means facing reality head on. On the road, that could look like adjusting your riding style for bad weather. In life, acceptance looks like acknowledging challenges, accepting them, and moving forward with a constructive mindset.

- *Reframing* is seeing obstacles from a different angle, transforming setbacks into opportunities. Whether it's a blocked road or a difficult situation in life, reframing allows you to find new paths and learning opportunities.

- *Take Action*, the final step, involves moving from thought to action, taking small steps to overcome obstacles rather than being paralysed by fear.

The CART model is more than a mental exercise. It's a practice that deepens with time and experience. Resilience grows each time we face adversity with awareness and action, just like a rider's skills develop with each kilometre travelled. Neuroscience tells us that resilience is linked to neuroplasticity, the brain's ability to adapt and rewire in response to experience.

An example of CART in action:

Overcoming her job loss

Background: Sarah, a coaching client of mine, was a mid-level manager in a national firm. She had been working her way up the corporate ladder for years. One day, she was unexpectedly laid off due to company downsizing. She was devastated and uncertain about the future, especially as she had financial commitments and no clear next steps in mind. However, we used the CART model in a coaching session to navigate the situation.

Commitment: Sarah first reminded herself of her core values and purpose. She had always been committed to personal growth and helping others succeed. Despite the setback, she vowed not to lose sight of those values. She committed to moving forward, focusing on building a future where she could continue growing her career, even if it meant starting from scratch.

Acceptance: The initial shock of the job loss was overwhelming, but Sarah chose to face the reality of the situation. Instead of denying or dwelling on her feelings of disappointment, she accepted them and recognised that sometimes life throws curveballs. She acknowledged that this was a setback, but it didn't define her or her future. She realised that to move forward, she needed to accept this change rather than resist it.

Reframing: Rather than seeing her job loss as a failure, Sarah reframed the situation as an opportunity. She asked herself, "What could I learn from this?" and "What opportunities lie within this situation?" She realised that this was a chance to pivot her career, possibly exploring a new industry or pursuing freelance work. She saw it as a step towards taking control of her career in a way she hadn't considered before.

Take Action: Sarah didn't waste time wallowing. She immediately updated her résumé, reconnected with her professional network, and sought out job opportunities that aligned with her reframed goals. She also enrolled in an online course to gain skills in a new field that interested her, and she started reaching out to former colleagues for advice and potential leads. By taking proactive steps, she took charge of her future instead of waiting for things to "get better" on their own.

Outcome: Within two months, Sarah had found a new job in a field she was passionate about. She also gained a deeper sense of confidence and resilience. The experience taught her that even in the face of adversity, the right mindset and approach – based on Commitment, Acceptance, Reframing, and Take Action – could help her emerge stronger and more aligned with her personal goals.

Everyone has tough times

Like everyone, in my life (and while riding, too), I've faced moments of self-doubt, fear and uncertainty. What got me through mine wasn't stoic toughness. It was perspective and taking responsibility. I would pause, take a breath and reframe, so I could remember what matters. That shift of mindset from reaction to intention is resilience. It's not just bouncing back from tough times; it's also about growing and developing so you're different at the end of the hard time.

Divorce, a financial loss, serious illness, the death of someone close and losing one's job are just a few examples of major setbacks that many people face. The way you respond to such events will indicate your level of resilience and your ability to move forward and create a more positive future in spite of what has happened.

Resilience is also a core principle in the Stoic and Zen philosophies, both of which emphasise acceptance, adaptability and inner strength when facing adversity. Stoics remind us that while we can't control external events, we can control how we respond to them. Zen philosophy, similarly, teaches that resisting hardship only creates suffering, whereas acceptance and adaptability allow us to move forward with clarity and purpose.

Resourcefulness: The skill to find a way

Resilience keeps us in the game, but sometimes we need more than just resilience. Sometimes we need resourcefulness, the skill to find creative solutions with what's at hand. When it comes to being resourceful, few fictional characters embody the trait quite like MacGyver from the classic 1980s TV series that was named after him. Faced with impossible situations, limited tools and always no time to spare, MacGyver consistently found clever, unconventional solutions using whatever was at hand, be it a penknife, paperclip, duct tape or a piece of string. His genius lay in his lateral thinking style. MacGyver's adventures reminded us that a resourceful person doesn't need all the right tools, all the answers, or perfect conditions. They stay calm, think creatively, and use what they have to move forward. In many ways, MacGyver mirrored the challenges of real life: when a plan falls apart, our ability to adapt and improvise will make the difference.

In a metaphysical sense, resourcefulness is not just about clever problem-solving; it is the art of stepping beyond appearances and aligning with the deeper rhythm of a situation. It mirrors the way a Zen archer approaches the bow: rather than straining to hit the target, the archer dissolves the boundary between self, bow, arrow, and target until the shot "shoots itself." In the same way, true resourcefulness comes when we stop forcing outcomes and instead attune ourselves to the underlying energy of the moment. The useful question becomes, *"What is this situation demanding of me?"* By loosening our grip on how things "should be," we open ourselves to how things actually are. From that place of presence, we discover a wider field of possibility and find solutions that would never appear if we were trapped in rigid thinking. Just as the arrow finds its mark when the archer steps aside, we tap into the infinite potential lying just beneath the surface when we allow resourcefulness to flow through us rather than forcing it from us.

The Interplay: Where resilience and resourcefulness meet

Think of resilience as the fuel that keeps the engine running and resourcefulness as the map and toolkit that help us get to where we're going. Without resilience, we give up too easily. Without resourcefulness, we stay stuck when we hit problems, no matter how determined we are. In a foggy Queensland mountain pass, for instance, resilience would be the ability to slow down and stay calm. Resourcefulness would be remembering an alternative route or finding a safe spot to wait for the fog to clear. Together, resilience and resourcefulness keep you moving through challenges, detours and obstacles.

As Henry David Thoreau stated, "Things do not change. We change." You're either growing or shrinking. Expanding or contracting. That's it. There is no status quo. Life is always in motion – and so must you be. If you want to thrive, not just survive, resourcefulness is non-negotiable. Don't wait. Don't wish. Work with what you've got.

Embracing failure as progress: A lesson from motorcycling and life

When asked about his thousands of failed attempts before inventing the lightbulb, Thomas Edison famously said, "I have not failed. I've just found 10,000 ways that don't work." This philosophy, rooted in resilience and resourcefulness, applies not only to invention but also to motorcycling and life itself.

Many people quit after one setback. Some after a handful. But those who achieve great things understand that progress is often wrapped in trial, error, perseverance and adaptability. Resilience means choosing belief over discouragement and progress over perfection. Focusing on what's possible, rather than what's gone wrong. Just like Edison, you don't have to get it right the first time. Being resourceful means you keep trying different things, even in the face of setbacks and "failures".

Motorcycling: Learning through experience

Like Edison's process of trial and error, motorcycling is an evolving journey. Every misjudged corner, unexpected detour or long, gruelling ride is an opportunity to improve. Mistakes aren't failures. They are lessons in control, focus and adaptability. Every mistake refines your skills. For example, a poorly executed turn teaches the importance of proper body positioning. A wrong route choice highlights the value of navigation skills and planning.

Life's harsh lessons: Weathering the storm

Australia's landscapes and weather are as unpredictable as life itself. One moment, the road is smooth and the skies clear. The next, a bushfire, flood, or dust storm changes everything. The harsh Australian climate has tested the resilience of its people for many generations going back thousands of years, yet Aussies of all types have always found ways to bounce back, rebuild and move forward.

Like a rider adjusting to sudden deterioration in the road surface, life sometimes demands quick thinking and resourcefulness. Farmers are a great example of this. When the worst storm in decades ruins their harvest, they will bounce back and start again. The ability to regroup and start over or pivot and find another path using different resources separates those who succeed from those who get stuck.

Whether it's losing a crop in a storm, losing everything in a fire, or facing some sort of personal adversity, Australians have an innate ability to push forward. Just as Edison saw every failure as progress, the Aussie spirit is about getting back on the bike, dusting off and continuing the ride.

Develop a CANI mindset

In 1991, while living in Auckland, New Zealand, I travelled to the US to attend several personal development seminars with Tony Robbins. That's where I first encountered the acronym CANI: Constant and Never-ending Improvement. CANI is both a philosophy and a habit. It means you keep learning, evolving and growing – no matter what. And to do that, you must be resourceful.

A potential disaster: A flat tyre on a quiet "C" road

While I was living in Melbourne, I spent several days riding solo around Victoria. Not long after heading inland from Lakes Entrance, I hit a long stretch of roadworks on a fairly isolated "C" road. Over five kilometres of slow riding on surfaces alternating between potholes and freshly laid gravel, made worse by a water truck spraying the gravel. Not the ideal conditions for a heavily laden street bike.

About halfway through, I felt the back of the bike go soft. A flat tyre. This was before the days of mobile phones. The road was quiet. The nearest road crew was about three kilometres back. It would've been easy to get frustrated or start to worry, but neither of those reactions would have fixed the tyre. Instead, I remembered that I had packed a tyre plug kit and a hand pump. I'd never used either before, but there I was, figuring it out on the side of the road. And figure it out I did.

That day, I didn't just fix a flat tyre. I learnt something far more valuable:

with the right mindset, a bit of ingenuity, and a touch of forward planning, you can work your way out of most situations. Even if it takes three times longer than it might for someone else. That's resourcefulness in action. You don't have to know everything. It's more important to trust yourself to figure things out when it matters. One of my personal beliefs is that there is no such thing as a problem without a gift for you in its hands.

The Stoics on resourcefulness

The Stoics would nod approval at a resourcefulness mindset. Epictetus taught that we should concern ourselves only with what is within our control – and resourcefulness is one of the things that we can control. He believed we always have power over how we respond, even when we can't control the situation. Marcus Aurelius wrote, "The impediment to action advances action. What stands in the way becomes the way." In other words, every obstacle is fuel for creativity and growth. When you meet hardship with resourcefulness, you will transform the problem into part of the path.

The Zen perspective

Similarly, the Zen tradition encourages us to embrace the present moment and respond with awareness. In Zen, resourcefulness is not frantic fixing; it's the calm, mindful use of what you have (remember MacGyver). It's letting go of the wish that things were different and simply *working with what is*, right now, without complaint or drama. As the Zen proverb goes, 'Before enlightenment, chop wood, carry water. After enlightenment, chop wood, carry water." Resourcefulness isn't glamorous. It's humble. It's just doing the next right thing, one thing at a time.

The cost of not being resourceful

When you're not resourceful, you'll inevitably become dependent on luck, other people, or on the vague hope that things will somehow "get better". But they don't. *You* get better, and then things get better. Waiting for your partner, your job, your boss, the government or your luck to change is giving away your power, and you will get old waiting. The better question is, "Who do I need to become to make this happen?" That is the mindset of a resourceful person.

Being resourceful can make you an expert in your chosen area

You'd be amazed at what you could achieve in just twelve months if you were resourceful. Let's say you wanted to become a confident public speaker, and your starting point is that the very thought of speaking in public terrifies you.

What if, over the next year, you were to:

- Read one book (or listen to an audio book) every month on public speaking, great speakers in history, and/or communication and persuasion. (Can't afford it? Go to the library.)

- Subscribe to YouTube channels, Facebook groups and podcasts on public speaking.

- Attend one "How to be a Great Public Speaker" seminar per quarter, virtually or in person.

- Join a Toastmasters group or a speaking club.

- Offer to speak for free at local clubs or schools.

- Find a speaking coach, even just for a few sessions.

Do that for a year, and you wouldn't just be "improved" – you'd be transformed. You'd be someone new. Do it for three years, double both your practice rate and your failure rate, and you would be transformed into a "Master Speaker". Mastery of anything comes from years of practice and learning through wins and failures. Take Picasso, for instance.

Picasso in Paris

When Pablo Picasso was an old man, a woman approached him in a Parisian café and asked him if he could do a quick drawing on a napkin for her. Picasso quickly sketched something and then handed it to her. But when she reached out to take it, he asked her for $20,000 to pay for it.

The woman was shocked. "But that took you only a few minutes!"

Picasso is said to have replied, "No, madame, it took me a lifetime."

The moral of this tale is about the value of a master's skill, experience and creative power. The value of a piece of art has little to do with the time it takes to create it. You too, can become a master of many things if you put in the time, energy and effort – and are willing to learn from your failures.

The motorcycle mirror

Motorcycling and life share a fundamental truth: progress comes through experience, not perfection. Mistakes, detours and challenges provide that experience. They're not signs of failure but markers of growth. Whether navigating a winding mountain road or overcoming personal hardship, the ability to learn, adjust and persist defines success. Thomas J. Watson, Sr., a former Chairman of IBM, was quoted as saying, "To succeed, double your failure rate." His philosophy was that those who failed more often were also the ones learning and improving at a faster rate. Edison's wisdom reminds us that every discarded failure moves us forward. The key is to stay on the journey, embrace each challenge, and trust that every experience, good or bad, is another step towards mastery.

When you see problems as a challenge and mistakes as learning opportunities, you feel empowered and more in control. You recognise that life is sometimes difficult, but through that difficulty, you can learn and grow. It's easy to persist on the smooth stretches, harder when the bends get tighter. Instead of persevering, many will look for an easy way out or get down and discouraged. Life can knock you down, but it's up to you if you allow it to knock you out!

Perhaps a personal transformation is needed

Transformation refers to a profound and contextual shift in a person's way of being, thinking, feeling and behaving. A "mind-quake", the effects of which ripple out in many directions. Unlike surface-level change such as adjusting habits or learning new skills, transformation shifts the core of who you are – your mindset, your identity, your beliefs and the way you see and engage with the world.

True transformation is usually triggered by meaningful life events, deliberate self-reflection, deep learning, or challenges that push you out of your comfort zone. It can also be sparked by a strong desire for growth, purpose or alignment with your values.

Pressure can lead to transformation

Diamonds are forged under immense pressure deep within the Earth's mantle. Pressure shapes humans too, pressing us into growth or cracking us apart. A motorcycle provides a powerful "vehicle" for this metaphor.

When you first climb onto a bike, especially a powerful one, it can feel like a beast beneath you: raw energy, momentum, force. The pressure is immediate. You must master balance, control speed, and wrestle with the discomfort of uncertainty. The intensity sharpens when riding a set of bends at speed: choosing your line, leaning at the right angle, braking, and accelerating out, all within seconds.

These physical and mental demands mirror the psychological pressures we all face. External expectations and demands, internal doubts, and unspoken fears push us to confront parts of ourselves we'd rather ignore. This is where we meet what Carl Jung called *the shadow*: the unconscious storehouse of traits and impulses we repress because they clash with our self-image.

Traditionally, this has been understood as the "dark shadow". This consists of qualities like anger, envy, shame or greed that feel socially or morally unacceptable. More recently, Jungian thinkers have added the idea of the "golden shadow": our hidden strengths, creativity, or brilliance that we disown because they feel too grand or threatening. In both cases, the parts we reject don't vanish; they are banished into the dark, and they create inner friction until we face them.

Integrating the shadow means acknowledging these hidden aspects. Not acting them out blindly but recognising them as real and reclaiming the energy spent denying them. In doing so, we move toward wholeness.

Just as leaning into a curve transforms pressure into flow, leaning into our own shadows, both dark and golden, turns discomfort into growth. As Jung wrote, "One does not become enlightened by imagining figures of light, but by making the darkness conscious. The latter procedure, however, is disagreeable and therefore not popular." Yet it is precisely in this meeting with the shadow that transformation, like a diamond under pressure, becomes possible.

Having explored the shadow, we now look at how it manifests both within ourselves and our interactions with others. This is where projection comes into play: the tendency to attribute our own hidden fears and desires to others, rather than owning them as part of our own experience.

The philosopher Ken Wilber talks extensively about shadow work and projection. If someone has a strong internal drive (say, ambition or assertiveness) but represses it because it conflicts with their self-image or values, that drive may appear in the world as "external pressure". Thus, "I want to do it," when repressed and projected, is experienced as "They are forcing me to do it."

Just as shadow work is a dance between understanding and integrating the parts of ourselves that we often deny or repress, motorcycling is a dance between control and letting go. Your body feels the strain when you push through a challenging turn, but the tension you feel helps you begin to find your rhythm. The more you embrace that tension, the more you can direct the bike with confidence. Similarly, as you face external pressures, whether from others or from within, you can choose to either resist them or use them to guide you towards growth and deeper self-awareness.

This is where the dark side, or shadow, comes in. Just as a rider must face and harness the force of the bike in difficult conditions, we too must face the shadow, unexamined parts of ourselves to move forward. Often, these are the fears, doubts and repressed desires that hold us back. When we repress them, they may show up as obstacles or external pressures that seem out of our control. But just as in riding, where pressure can be a force for transformation, facing our inner darkness can propel us towards our full potential, shaping us into the person we are meant to be.

Transformation involves moving beyond old limitations, the outdated stories you tell yourself, or unconscious patterns and stepping into a more authentic, aware and empowered version of yourself. More than fixing something broken, transformation involves unfolding your deeper potential and evolving through experiences, insights and conscious choices.

The science of transformation: The theory of dissipative structures

In 1977, the Russian-born Belgian chemist Ilya Prigogine was awarded the Nobel Prize in Chemistry for his pioneering work in non-equilibrium thermodynamics, particularly his theory of dissipative structures. His research showed how certain systems, when driven far from equilibrium, can reorganise into higher levels of order and complexity. Though Prigogine's work was rooted in chemistry and physics, its insights have since been applied metaphorically to personal growth, resilience, and thriving under pressure.

Open and Closed Systems

In nature, there are two broad types of systems: closed and open.

- A closed system is isolated from its environment, exchanging neither matter nor energy with the outside world. Over time, closed systems drift towards disorder (entropy). A thermos of hot coffee is a rough approximation: once sealed, the system slowly loses energy but has little interaction with its surroundings.

- An open system, by contrast, continually exchanges energy and matter with its environment. Open systems are capable of self-organisation and evolution into more complex forms. A living organism, for instance, takes in oxygen and nutrients, processes them to fuel metabolism, and expels waste products.

Prigogine extended this concept beyond biology. A town, for example, is an open system. It imports electricity, water, and raw materials; uses them in homes, offices, and factories; and exports goods, services, and waste. Likewise, a company draws in resources, transforms them, and adapts continually to external pressures.

How Dissipative Structures Work

A dissipative structure is a special type of open system that does not collapse under stress. Instead, when pushed far from equilibrium, it enters a phase of instability, then reorganises into a new, more complex state.

A simple illustration is boiling water. As heat energy increases, the water molecules move chaotically. But at a threshold, the system doesn't dissolve into disorder; it undergoes a phase transition, forming convection currents, and a new, ordered pattern emerges from chaos.

In life, the same principle applies. Stress, setbacks, or disruption can feel overwhelming, yet they often create the very conditions for growth. When we adapt effectively, we don't return to our old "normal." We evolve into more resilient, resourceful versions of ourselves.

Dissipative Structures and Human Transformation

People are open systems. We take in food, air, ideas, and experiences and transform them into action, creativity, and meaning. When stress, conflict, or change push us off balance, we enter instability, and this is precisely when transformation becomes possible.

- Crisis as a catalyst: Personal crises, whether in relationships, work, or health, often force us to abandon the familiar. By embracing the disruption instead of resisting it, we emerge with new skills, insights and resilience.

- Resilience and adaptation: Just as nature reorganises under pressure, so too can we. Those who thrive use adversity as fuel for reinvention.

- The power of letting go: Sometimes the old structure must collapse before the new one can form. Clinging to outdated beliefs or behaviours keeps us stuck. Transformation requires surrender to change.

Prigogine's theory reveals a profound truth: instability and pressure are not inherently destructive. They are the mechanisms of evolution. Growth rarely comes from comfort. More often, it comes from being tested, disrupted, and reorganised into something greater.

Breakdown or Breakthrough?

The choice is ours. By welcoming change rather than resisting it, we can transform life pressures and even crises into stepping stones. If we link pain only to pressure, we may collapse. If, instead, we link possibility and growth to pressure, we will keep pushing through until we reach breakthrough. As Tony Robbins observes, "What you link pain and pleasure to will shape your destiny."

Pressure and Transformation in Motorcycling

Motorcycling offers a visceral metaphor for this principle. Riding constantly places us in dialogue with pressure, balancing, adapting and adjusting in response to road, weather and speed. The act of cornering at pace is a perfect example: instability feels threatening at first, yet leaning into it is the only way to ride smoothly through the curve.

Prigogine himself noted in his Nobel lecture that "non-equilibrium may become a source of order, and irreversible processes may lead to a new type of dynamic states of matter." On the road, those moments when the bike feels unstable are also the moments when a rider's control, focus and resilience are forged.

Carl Jung put it succinctly: "Crisis is what happens when the old system can no longer bear the pressure." On a motorcycle, as in life, crisis is both a test and an invitation to adapt, to reorganise, and to emerge stronger.

In the end, resilience and resourcefulness are not just survival traits; they are pathways to wholeness. Every challenge, every bend in the road, is an invitation to grow into our truest selves. To lean into the curve is to trust the hidden order of life, and in that trust, every ride becomes a journey of profound discovery.

Chapter 8:

COURAGE, RISK AND COMMITMENT

Every rider knows this moment. The road curves unexpectedly tightly. Blind, and sharper than it looked on approach. Your body tenses. Instinct (and Crocky) whispers, "Straighten up. Ease off. Play it safe." But the experienced biker knows the truth. Survival lies in the lean and in smooth acceleration. You don't resist the curve. You flow into it. You trust the bike, your training, your experience and, most of all, your commitment.

You lean in.

In that moment, the roar of the motorcycle and the rush of wind capture something essential: a life lived with courage, the acceptance of risk, and an unwavering commitment to the journey. These qualities – courage to face fear, willingness to take risks and commitment to keep going – come naturally to those who ride. As Helen Keller wrote in *The Open Door*, "Avoiding danger is no safer in the long run than outright exposure. The fearful are caught as often as the bold. Life is either a daring adventure or nothing." For many, riding a motorcycle is one such daring adventure. It's an experience that demands stepping out of comfort zones and into the unknown, where every twist of the throttle represents a choice to embrace life fully rather than hold back.

Courage and fear: The rider's heart into the unknown

Fear is one of the tools Crocky uses to keep dysfunctional internal chatter going and to keep you small. Fear is a major barrier to entering the flow state, and it hinders mindfulness and generally blocks personal development. Fear isn't the enemy, but it must be approached with the right mindset and with

Courage, Risk and Commitment

courage. Courage is action despite fear. Better yet, it's action *because* of fear. Courage manifests when you face the fear head on and transcend it through awareness and acceptance. You can reframe fear by viewing it as a challenge, and courage helps you rise to that challenge – fear and all.

Courage doesn't always appear as a knight in shining armour. More often, it's quiet, grounded and deeply personal. It's that quiet, deliberate choice to keep riding when doubt creeps in, perhaps when the wind picks up or the road is unfamiliar, or when past crashes still linger in your mind. Courage is making a bold career move when everyone around you advises caution. Courage is quitting a career that you are desperately unhappy in. It's choosing growth over comfort, even when the path forward feels uncertain. Taking responsibility for your choices and facing uncomfortable truths. You need courage to have the difficult conversation that you've been putting off for too long – the conversation that could mend a relationship, clarify boundaries, or set you free. Courage is signing up for that training course that intimidates you, starting the book you've always dreamed of writing, or walking away from a relationship that no longer aligns with who you are becoming. It's finally going on that long ride that you've dreamed about for years. It's turning "Someday I will" and "I'm gonna" into action.

Sometimes, courage is getting back on the bike after a fall, literally or metaphorically. Standing up, brushing off the dust, and deciding not to let the fear of failure dictate the rest of your journey. This happened to me recently. I was riding off from my mechanic's workshop and crossed a railway line at a bad angle. In a millisecond, I was on the ground watching my R1250RT skid towards a line of traffic. Thanks to my airbag, I wasn't hurt (except for my pride). And, luckily, the traffic was stopped at a red light. People jumped out of their cars to help, and within five minutes, I was up on my bike and headed back to the mechanic to check the damage to the bike.

This incident reinforced to me that true courage is far more accessible and is needed far more often in daily life than simply in extreme situations like a fire walk or riding through the outback solo. True courage leans into the fear, even when the fear is loud. Fear rarely disappears, but each time you act despite it, your courage will grow stronger. And it will become a habit. A way of showing up in the world with clarity, conviction and heart.

On two wheels, fear can be useful, even a basic survival mechanism, but when left unchecked, fear shrinks our world. It causes hesitation and indecision – dangerous when on a bike. We pull back and automatically bring our energy into our centre to help us feel safe. Psychologists tell us that fear narrows our field of vision, reduces our sensory perception and tightens our awareness. When we most need to be open, agile and aware, fear causes us to contract. It closes doors. And unless we do something deliberate to break that pattern, it will lead straight into affecting other areas of life. As Seneca wrote: "Sometimes even to live is an act of courage."

I've experienced fear, and I've also seen riders who fear risk, avoid challenge and stay in their comfort zones. But those who avoid challenge stay stuck. And those who avoid growth settle for far less than they're capable of. As Thomas Edison once said, "If we all did the things we are capable of doing, we would literally astound ourselves."

The great tragedy

Most people never find out what they're truly capable of, not because they lack talent, intelligence or opportunity, but because fear gets the final say and inertia sets in (remember the forces of expansion and contraction discussed in Chapter 3). Fear, ventriloquising through Crocky, whispers the worst-case scenario and convinces them that discomfort is danger. It builds walls where there were only open doors. It stops people from starting, from speaking up, from risking, from leaning into the curve.

And, so, unless they over compensate and develop a sort of superiority complex and think there is not only the best way, but the only way, fearful people tend to play small. They stick to the roads they've outgrown. They opt for comfort over growth. Familiarity over fulfilment.

Typical fear-based behaviour includes:

- Laughing nervously
- Withdrawing emotionally
- Drinking alcohol and/or taking unnecessary drugs
- Freezing
- Getting angry at somebody who has nothing to do with one's fear
- Going quiet
- Going shopping
- Catastrophic fantasising and imagining everything else that could go wrong in one's life.

But the real risk for a fearful person is regret, not failure. Deep down, a part of them knows that they could have become bolder, braver, more alive. And that's the heartbreak Not that they couldn't, but that they *didn't*. Australian author and speaker Bronnie Ware, who spent years caring for patients in their final days, says the most common regret of the dying that she heard was this: "I wish I'd had the courage to live a life true to myself, not the life others expected of me." *So* often, this regret reflects opportunities not taken, chances missed due to fear. In contrast, those who embrace calculated risks often end up with richer stories to tell, and they are haunted by fewer "what ifs".

Living your potential after extreme hardship

Living your potential doesn't only mean uncovering hidden talents or pursuing passions that come easily. It's often the result of being willing to accept discomfort. Stepping into life's unknown corners with courage, grappling with risk and making the unwavering commitment to grow, even when everything feels like it's falling apart.

Polish psychologist Kazimierz Dąbrowski, who worked closely with survivors of the Second World War, saw firsthand how some of the most resilient people had transformed their suffering into strength. Through his theory of "positive disintegration", Dąbrowski argued that when a person's familiar world collapsed, when the structures that once felt secure to them crumbled, they were forced to confront themselves and decide whether to retreat or lean into the challenge with courage. Such a decision is a breakdown or breakthrough point.

Dąbrowski found that many war survivors didn't just endure; they reshaped and reinvented themselves, forging new identities from the ashes of their suffering. Some became doctors or teachers or advocates, devoting their lives to helping others. They chose to face the scary uncertainty of building new lives despite their trauma, fear and pain, and they committed themselves to something greater than themselves.

Imagine a concentration camp prisoner who chose, despite the odds, to keep composing poems of resistance. Krystyna Żywulska, for instance, risked everything by memorising her poems and passing them on so her story stayed alive. She committed herself not only to survival but also to ensuring her words might one day shine a light for others lost in darkness. Her postwar works documented her suffering but also carried a fierce compassion that inspired countless others to reflect on their own humanity. That is the essence of living your potential: taking a stand when it would have been easier to hide or remain silent.

I sometimes wonder how it was for my father after four years in a German POW camp. What courage did it take for him to step back into the world, to build a life out of the fragments of war? Did he feel that the road he'd known had been completely washed away, leaving only the chance to create a new one? I suspect he did, but, like many who returned from those horrors of war, he never spoke about it. And because I was only nine years old when he died, I never got the chance to ask him.

This is the lesson for all of us: the path to potential is rarely paved in comfort. It demands risk. It calls for courage to enter the unknown terri-

Courage, Risk and Commitment

tory of the new. It requires us to risk letting go of who we were, face the unknown, and dare to believe we can become someone stronger, wiser and more compassionate. The path to potential is a brave one; to take that path, we must be willing to confront our own darkness and accept that pain can teach as well as wound. And it rewards commitment, a steady throttle of determination that keeps us moving forward, even when the road ahead is shrouded in fog.

In our own lives, we may not face the same unimaginable horrors of war, but the principle remains: struggle, pain, and even breakdowns can become gateways to transformation. The road is rarely smooth, but getting around each obstacle we encounter can sharpen us and, in the process, teach us who we truly are, what our values are, and what we stand for.

Like a motorcyclist leaning into a curve, you must trust yourself and trust life, knowing that every bend is an invitation to grow, stretch and test your limits. Because that's what living your potential is all about: courageously embracing life's risks and staying committed to the journey, even when the outcome isn't certain.

So, the next time life throws you a challenge that feels too big to handle, take your chance to lean in, take a deep breath and learn. Your chance to ride into your potential.

On a motorcycle, risk is not an abstract concept. You can feel it in the tightening of your grip as you cross a high bridge buffeted by strong side winds or in the heightened awareness required when riding at night. But along with the danger comes a heightened sense of being alive.

Fear isn't to be avoided. It's there to be understood and responded to in different ways. At its core, fear is a primal biological response signalling potential danger. It screams, "Pay attention! Something here could harm you!" Riding teaches this lesson viscerally. Each time you roll on, you make a pact with risk. You accept the possibility of harm in exchange for the vivid reality of *living*. It's not that riders have a death wish. Far from it. What they have is a *life wish*: a desire to experience life keenly. In the words of Burt Munro, the legendary New Zealand motorcycle racer: "You live more in five minutes on a bike going flat out than some people live in a lifetime."

Burt Munro and The World's Fastest Indian

Burt Munro, born in Invercargill in the deep south of New Zealand, grew up with a passion for speed that turned into an unshakeable determination to build the fastest motorcycle in the world. **Courage** was the bedrock of his journey and resourcefulness and resilience were vital to his success. When most men his age were settling into quiet retirement, Munro refused to yield to the limitations of time or doubt. He was in his sixties when he took on the Bonneville Salt Flats in Utah, a place where only the bravest racers dared to test their machines and themselves. Despite other people's criticism and scepticism, and facing multiple obstacles, from mechanical failures to cost blowouts, he kept forging ahead, usually with a grin and the steely resolve that can only come from true courage.

Risk defined his life. Munro's bike, a heavily modified 1920 Indian Scout, was a machine that had been constructed in a Southland shed with ingenuity and inventiveness rather than high-tech engineering. The risks he took weren't only mechanical; he also faced the very real danger of serious injury or even death every time he opened the throttle on the salt.

Commitment fuelled Munro's dream. He spent decades perfecting his bike, crafting homemade pistons in his shed and testing them on the backroads of Invercargill. He invested everything into his vision. Even when funds ran dry or setbacks came thick and fast, he kept going. His life became a testament to the idea that commitment means giving your all, even when success seems distant.

In 1967, at the age of sixty-eight and on a forty-seven-year-old bike, Munro set a world record at Bonneville – 295.453 kph – a record for a motorcycle under 1,000cc that still stands today. (In fact, thanks to his son John's eagle eye in noticing a mathematical error had been made in calculating the speed, 37 years later, the record was updated to 296.259 kph.) His story reminds us that true achievement rarely comes without fear, uncertainty and sacrifice, but it's in facing those challenges head on with resilience and resourcefulness that greatness is born.

Stoic perspectives on courage and fear

But how do we face existential fear without letting it overwhelm us? Courage. Stoicism teaches that courage isn't about the absence of fear but the ability to act despite it. Marcus Aurelius wrote that external events aren't what disturb us; our judgements about them are what cause us problems. According to the Stoics, we can't control life's uncertainties, but we can control how we respond – ideally, with wisdom, acceptance and steady resolve.

Stoicism reminds us that courage doesn't mean never being afraid. Courage faces life's uncertainties with steady mind and open heart. Just as we lean into a curve instead of fighting it, we can lean into fear and uncertainty, finding our balance in the very act of riding through them.

Fear is often misunderstood. It's not a wall. Rather, it's a signpost and an opportunity to grow. It provides an opportunity to transcend old patterns and evolve behaviourally and spiritually. It often shows us where the gold is buried – what we fear most is often where the greatest gold lies. The fear of personal change, of letting go of who we were to become who we might be, is perhaps the most common fear of all. If we evade that change, we end up stuck in what I described earlier as the Valley of Reasons and Excuses.

Avoiding change is familiar. It's safe. And it leads to the slow death of potential.

The fire walk

When I was living in New Zealand and facilitating large personal development workshops, I had the honour of leading over 2,500 people through fire walks. There's nothing quite like walking barefoot across five metres of glowing, red-hot coals to get you focused. Fire walking is not a stunt. Taking the first step onto a bed of hot coals goes against every instinct we have. We must override Crocky and our body's urge to panic. We need to take a breath, focus our energy, and then step out.

What I saw those nights was profound. Here were people who had lived small lives for fear of failure or judgement suddenly doing something they never believed they could. The decision to take the first step was the real challenge, not the coals. But once they did, everything changed for them, because that's what courage and commitment do. It redefined what those people believed was possible. And some twenty-five years later, people are still drawing on their experience. Just earlier this year, one such participant commented to me that their fire walk had changed their life.

Riding a motorcycle and fire walking share this truth: the moment you show courage and truly commit, fear has nowhere left to grow. That's how courage works. I've said it before: doubt, fear and hesitation are dangerous on a motorcycle. Entering a curve half-heartedly will throw your bike off balance. You will wobble, tighten, panic. Commitment isn't reckless; it's stable. Decisive. Life is like that, too. Half-measures, hedged bets and "maybe later" are how dreams dissolve. As author and motivational speaker Jim Rohn put it, "Without a sense of urgency, desire loses its value."

You don't need to ride into the outback at night or walk on fire to be brave. But you do need to lean in. Fear rarely goes away, but courage grows when you act despite fear. Experienced bikers capture this balance with wry sayings. For example, American stuntman Evel Knievel famously noted, "There are old bikers and there are bold bikers, but there are no old, bold bikers." In other words, courage on a motorcycle must be tempered with respect for the risks.

Courage, Risk and Commitment

The great tragedy? Letting fear have the final say

Many people never find out what they're truly capable of. And not because they lack talent, intelligence or opportunity. It's because fear gets the final say. Fear, often expressed through the inner voice of Crocky, convinces them that discomfort is danger and uncertainty is a stop sign. It builds walls where there could be open doors. It stops them from starting, from speaking up, from risking. From leaning into the curve.

Charley Boorman chose differently

We met Charley Boorman in Chapter 1. A UK adventurer, TV presenter, and long-time friend and riding partner of the actor Ewan McGregor, Boorman has faced fear in its rawest form. In 2016, during a test ride in Portugal, Boorman collided head on with a car. The accident left him with a shattered left tibia and fibula and a broken right femur. It was a catastrophic crash that could have ended not just his career but also his passion. He spent months in hospital, endured multiple surgeries, and was told he would likely never ride again.

But Charley Boorman got back on the bike.

And not just once. He suffered another serious break in a later fall. But, yet again, he returned. Slowly. Deliberately. Courageously. His body was held together with titanium, but his spirit was intact. Boorman didn't return to the road because he was fearless. He returned because he refused to let fear dictate the boundaries of his life.

That's courage. And passion.

Courage isn't always obvious. Sometimes, it's the quiet decision to try again, when everything inside you (and other people) screams, "Don't!" Courage also means taking risks and, yes, sometimes failing. But as I've told every rider I've ever helped train, there's always an alternative path. There's always another route, another way forward – if you have the courage to look for it.

Playing it safe might avoid discomfort, but it's a prescription for a grey, dreary life.

As Ayn Rand wrote in *The Fountainhead*, "Throughout the centuries there were men who took first steps down new roads armed with nothing but their own vision." That takes courage. The kind of courage that doesn't wait for ideal conditions. The kind that acts in the presence of fear – not its absence. It's:

- Applying for the job even after many rejections and despite your confidence being shaken.
- Walking away from the relationship that's eroding you.
- Enrolling in that course. Making that call. Taking the first step.
- Getting back on the bike after a crash.

You don't need to be fearless. You need to act even though you're still afraid. Fake it till you become it! That's the only way you'll ever discover just how far you can go.

The English poet Christopher Logue captured it beautifully in his call to leap:

> Come to the edge.
>
> We might fall.
>
> Come to the edge.
>
> It's too high!
>
> COME TO THE EDGE!
>
> And they came.
>
> And he pushed.
>
> And they flew.

Risk: Dancing with danger

Risk comes hand in hand with courage. To ride is to accept risk. In fact, to live fully is to accept risk. It's undeniable that motorcycling carries greater dangers than many other daily activities. You're exposed to the elements and the carelessness of distracted drivers. Yet ask any passionate rider why they ride, and they'll likely echo the sentiment that the thrill and freedom of the ride is worth the risk. There is something profoundly enlivening about choosing a path that isn't the safest. As Richard Branson has said on numerous occasions, "The brave may not live forever, but the cautious never live at all."

Motorcycling has taught me many things over the decades, but perhaps this, most of all: you can't control the road, but you *can* control the lean. As W. Mitchell said, "It's not what happens to you, it's what you do about it." And the ones who thrive in both riding and life are the ones who lean in rather than pull out. Crucially, courage often begins with a single decision: to turn up and give it a go.

What about motivation?

You don't have to feel invincible or "ready" to start. As a biker friend put it, "You don't have to be fearless. You don't have to be perfect. You just have to be willing." Typically, people think that motivation comes before action, when, in reality, it's the other way around. Action precedes motivation. In fact, those who wait to be motivated will often do nothing apart from watching as the window of opportunity slams shut. Rather than waiting for a burst of motivation to, well, motivate you, take action – even a small step is better than doing nothing. Taking one small step will then motivate you to take another. Relying on feeling motivated sets you up for failure. Committed, disciplined action in line with your values will help you achieve and become almost anything you want to achieve and become.

Motorcycling teaches this lesson in real time: when faced with a bend in the road or a sudden gust of wind, you don't wait for perfect confidence –

you lean in, commit, and let your experience catch up. That's action creating motivation. If you can face down literal storms on a bike, suddenly that difficult conversation or daunting life change seems a little less frightening. The motorcycle, as Pirsig observed in *Zen and the Art of Motorcycle Maintenance*, is as much mental as mechanical: "That's all the motorcycle is, a system of concepts worked out in steel. ...the motorcycle is primarily a mental phenomenon." In mastering the machine and the road, you're really mastering yourself – your anxieties, your focus, your resolve. This is the rider's heart: courage as self-mastery, forged in the crucible of wind and speed.

Whatever curveball life throws at you, trust yourself and lean into it.

The power of commitment

If courage gets you started, then commitment is what keeps you going. It's the backbone of every meaningful pursuit, the glue that holds your goals together when the initial inspiration fades and reality bites.

Commitment is often misunderstood. People think it's about motivation, that spark of enthusiasm one might feel at the beginning of a project. But motivation is fleeting. Commitment is the deeper force that keeps you going after any initial burst of motivation wears off. It's the decision you make repeatedly – every morning, every setback, every detour.

Motorcycling teaches this with raw clarity. Anybody can get excited about a ride on a sunny day. But commitment is what sees you through crosswinds, fatigue, unexpected detours or rain lashing your visor for three hours straight. It's what drives you to prep your bike properly, plan your route, and keep going when the fun has faded and all that's left is distance to travel and discomfort. It's what gets you back in the saddle after a near miss, a mechanical failure or a moment of doubt.

More than once, I've found myself hours into a long day's ride, bone tired, nowhere near the next town – let alone my planned destination for that day – and questioning every decision that got me there. And yet, I kept going.

Why? Because I'd committed. The goal wasn't negotiable. The discomfort wasn't permanent. And at the end of the day – literally – the sense of integrity, of finishing what I had started, was worth more than the temporary struggle.

Commitment or interest

In a world of quick fixes, interest is easy. Commitment is rare. Interest is the spark that gets you started, but commitment is the steady flame that keeps you going. Committed riders turn out in any weather, on any road, with unwavering resolve. Commitment isn't conditional; it's a promise you make to yourself to keep going, even when it's uncomfortable. Commitment transforms fleeting interest into meaningful action.

Scottish mountaineer and writer W.H. Murray sums up commitment beautifully:

> Until one is committed, there is hesitancy, the chance to draw back, always ineffectiveness. Concerning all acts of initiative (and creation), there is one elementary truth the ignorance of which kills countless ideas and splendid plans: that the moment one definitely commits oneself, then Providence moves too. All sorts of things occur to help one that would never otherwise have occurred. A whole stream of events issues from the decision, raising in one's favour all manner of unforeseen incidents, meetings and material assistance, which no man could have dreamt would have come his way.

Commitment is a catalyst for synchronicity

Commitment is a key that unlocks synchronicity. When you have a clear intention and commitment to a goal or path of action, seemingly random but meaningful coincidences occur that are aligned with your intention - events, people and opportunities "coincidentally" turn up. It's as if the universe rewards your commitment with synchronistic moments - the right person at the next petrol stop, the hidden gem of a café just when you need a break, the perfect patch of tarmac at just the right time. Commitment opens the road, and the road answers.

When you're committed, you find a way. When you're merely interested, you'll find reasons and excuses not to follow through. Commitment sustains effort through challenges, and it draws opportunities into your orbit.

The physics of motorcycling

Enter a corner with doubt and a lack of commitment, and your bike will become unstable. A half-lean is worse than none. The physics of motorcycling is straightforward: commitment creates stability. The same applies in life. Half-hearted efforts lead to shaky outcomes. But when you commit fully – mentally, emotionally, physically – then things will click. You enter a state of flow. You build trust in yourself. You gather momentum.

And momentum, once it has been built, becomes its own kind of magic. You stop negotiating with yourself. You stop questioning. You just ride.

Commitment is when there's alignment between what you say matters and what you actually do. It's a form of personal integrity. And it's one of the most empowering traits you can cultivate.

Commitment transforms fear into fuel

Something remarkable happens when you commit fully: fear loses its grip. When you decide there's no turning back, your energy stops splintering in multiple directions. Doubt quietens. Focus sharpens. You move forwards with clarity and power. This is what I saw again and again in fire walking. People who hesitated, who approached the coals with one foot out the door, often wobbled or got burnt. You could see the doubt on their faces. But those who locked in – with presence, intent and commitment – walked clean and uninjured. The fire didn't change. Their mindset did.

The same psychology of commitment applies to motorcycling. The road is what it is: unpredictable, sometimes unforgiving. But your relationship to it changes the moment you say, "I'm in. Fully." When you do that, the fear won't disappear, but it will no longer steer. It's no longer in charge.

Commitment leads to success

I use a simple formula for success with my coaching clients:

$$\textbf{Vision} \\ + \\ \textbf{Passion} \\ + \\ \textbf{Courage} \\ + \\ \textbf{Action} \\ = \\ \textbf{Success.}$$

There's a beautiful simplicity to it. Vision + Passion + Courage + Action = Success. Yet behind its elegance lies something deeper, a powerful truth. Whether you're setting off on a long motorcycle tour, chasing a personal dream, or navigating a life transition, this formula holds up. But there's a hidden gear that makes the whole machine move - commitment. Without commitment, passion flickers, vision blurs and action stalls.

Let's break this down, as understanding each element is essential. Because every part needs to work together.

Vision: The map that guides

Vision gives passion a direction. It's your roadmap. Whether you're crossing a continent, building a career or raising a family. Vision transforms a vague desire into a focused plan. On the road, vision is knowing where you're headed; not only the destination but also the experience you want to have along the way. Will you ride coastal or mountain? Cruise or challenge?

Without vision, you might still move, but you'll be wandering. In life, vision lets you choose not only what you want but also who you want to become.

Passion: The spark that ignites

The spark that ignites. Every great ride begins with passion, that inner fire that draws you to the open road. It's what makes your heart race as you check the weather, pack the panniers or fuel up before dawn. In life, passion is the emotional fuel that gets you started. It gives meaning to your goals and provides energy when Crocky might say, "Why bother?"

But passion alone isn't enough. You can love riding and still never leave the driveway. You can dream big and still not take the first step.

Courage: The heart of a meaningful life

Courage is at the heart of a full and meaningful life, and this includes being a key factor in mental health. It begins with the courage to be imperfect; to admit that you don't have it all together, yet you still choose to show up. Life is uncertain, but when you engage with it courageously despite your doubts, fears and flaws, you unlock the possibility of growth and contribution.

Courage is also needed to move towards success. It's about stepping into the unknown, beyond the comfortable edges of life. It's what allows you to take risks, to stretch into new challenges, and to discover abilities you didn't know you had. That moment of leaning into fear is often the very place where creativity, performance, and transformation occur. Without it, life becomes flat. With it, life expands.

At the same time, courage is the backbone of maturity and integrity. Sooner or later, everybody has problems and encounters pain. Sometimes the bigger problem is not having the courage to take responsibility. To become truly successful, truths – sometimes hard-to-face truths – need to be faced. And that takes courage. Turning away only breeds stagnation and regret. Facing reality directly requires courage, but it also brings depth, resilience and authenticity. It makes love stronger, choices clearer and living more honest.

Courage doesn't eliminate fear, and it doesn't make life easier. What it does is give life richness. It allows us to embrace imperfection, to reach for growth, and to face reality as it is. In doing so, it opens the door to a life that is not just endured but truly lived.

Committed Action: The throttle that moves you forward

Then comes action. You can have the dream bike, the maps, and all the right gear, but until you twist the throttle, you're not going anywhere. Action is where the rubber meets the road. It's the habit of getting up early to train, learn, ride, write or work, no matter what the weather is and even when you don't feel like it.

Motorcyclists know this well: commitment to regular maintenance matters. So do preparation and planning. Once you get moving, the road will test you with potholes, rain, crazy drivers, fatigue, breakdowns. And this is where commitment shows up.

Commitment: The glue that holds it all together

Commitment is the backbone. Without commitment, passion fades when the initial excitement wears off. Vision becomes a wish list. Action stops at the first sign of discomfort. Commitment gets you back in the saddle after a rough day. It keeps you going when the ride is long, the wind is strong and the road turns to gravel. It chooses to lean in rather than pull back.

Commitment separates tourists from travellers, dabblers from doers. When the weather shifts; when the plan unravels; when you're cold, hungry or mentally spent. Commitment is what keeps you going.

In life, it's no different. Success and happiness rarely arrive in a straight line. They come through a clear vision, persistence and adaptation. And showing up. Again, and again.

Roadside Reflection

There have been days when the ride was pure flow. Blue skies, sweeping bends and a steady rhythm. But I've also had days where everything went wrong. Missed turns, unexpected detours, and pouring rain with headwinds that made me question why I had even started. On those days, I remembered my identity as a motorcyclist and fortified myself by remembering these things:

- I had a route in mind – a reason and a vision.
- I started this ride today because I love riding. That's passion.
- I was on the road. I was taking action.
- And the fact that I kept going? Commitment.

Success at anything isn't an accident. It's the result of a commitment.

The bricklayer's commitment

This classic story illustrates commitment beautifully:

> A man was walking past a construction site where three bricklayers were hard at work. Curious, he asked each one the same question: "What are you doing?"
>
> The first bricklayer answered, "I'm laying bricks." The second replied, "I'm building a wall." But the third bricklayer paused, with a spark in his eye, then said, "I'm building a cathedral."

That third bricklayer wasn't just laying bricks; he was part of a grand vision. His commitment extended beyond the task at hand to the legacy he was helping to create. He understood that every brick he placed, no matter how ordinary, was contributing to something extraordinary.

Commitment works the same way in life. Grinding through each day, detached from purpose, is not commitment. Commitment is seeing your efforts as part of a larger mission, a cathedral of your own making. When you know the "why" behind your work, you're more likely to endure the challenges, stay focused and keep giving your best even when progress feels slow.

Commitment is the fuel that keeps you going. The sense that what you're doing matters and that every small step is a step to something much greater.

Build your cathedral

Success is built, not wished for. It's the product of aligned passion, clear vision and relentless action. But all of these things will only endure because of one thing: commitment.

The next time you're midway through a long ride or a project and you're physically and mentally stretched, ask yourself, "Why did I begin?" Let that question anchor you. Then lean into the next curve and enjoy the ride.

Because the real destination isn't a place. It's who you become on the ride.

Self-belief and mental toughness

In addition to skill and planning, success requires self-belief. Mental toughness helps a rider to face an unpredictable storm or a steep climb and say, "I've got this." This sort of inner dialogue quietens Crocky, pushes past doubt, trusts preparation, and chooses courage over comfort. Every rider has encountered moments where quitting would have felt easier. But belief in one's ability, even when the road is rough, is the foundation of resilience.

Delayed gratification: Playing the long game

Motorcycling, like life, often involves going through discomfort today for a payoff tomorrow. Long rides can mean early mornings, missed comforts and sore muscles, but we riders know the reward is well worth it. In life, those who master delayed gratification, who don't get distracted by the newest, brightest and shiniest thing, and who can say no to all manner of diversions for a greater future reward – they are the ones who achieve meaningful success and experience true happiness. Whether it's saving for your dream bike, working on your craft or building a business, patience is more than a virtue. In our instant-gratification, "I-must-have-it-now" world, I see patience as a sort of superpower.

Emotional investment: Riding with your heart

To have the courage to take risks and commit to something, you have to care. Emotional investment means you've put your heart into the ride, the goal, the relationship or the mission. It keeps you connected to your purpose when Crocky says, "Turn back." Passion fuels you, but emotional investment binds you to the outcome. You're more than just "in it" – you're all in!

The most powerful drive comes from within. The desire to grow, to master something, to fulfil a personal goal is what makes the journey meaningful – that's *intrinsic motivation*. Intrinsic motivation is an "inside job". It might be influenced by external factors, but deep-seated intrinsic motivation keeps you going when the going gets tough. No applause, pay slip or praise can substitute for that deep internal satisfaction of doing something because you love it. Motorcyclists don't ride for spectators or external accolades. They ride for the feeling. Likewise, in life, success built on intrinsic motivation is sustainable, deeply satisfying and authentic.

Chapter 9

PURPOSE, PASSION AND THE POWER OF CLEAR DIRECTION

"

Those who have a 'why' to live, can bear with almost any how
- Viktor Frankl -

When psychologists Edward Deci and Richard Ryan met in 1977, the conversation they had led to a collaboration over decades and the development of the Self-Determination Theory (SDT) of motivation, which changed the way we understand human motivation.

Motivation had long been defined as merely "the energy required for action", and the prevailing wisdom was that the best way to get people to accomplish tasks was through external rewards such as money, praise or status. But Deci and Ryan turned that thinking on its head. They found that, whereas external incentives can work in the short term, real, lasting motivation – the kind that drives people to do their best and feel truly alive – comes from within a person. Intrinsic motivation is fuelled by passion and purpose, not obligation or applause.

As Ryan put it, "We've always been interested in factors that facilitate or undermine motivation, and in investigating that, we came on the idea that there are some basic psychological needs that everybody has, that help them thrive and have their highest quality motivation. Those basic psychological needs are autonomy, competence and relatedness. That's the theory in a nutshell."

Motorcyclists understand this intuitively. As previously stated, we don't ride because it's practical or logical. We ride because it calls to something deep inside us. That's intrinsic motivation. That's purpose. The more aligned we are with our inner compass, the more alive we feel. But when we're not, when we chase someone else's definition of success or ignore our own truth, life can start to feel like a ride with no map, no direction and no fuel.

The open road doesn't just take you places, it reveals why you're here.

Over five decades and hundreds of thousands of kilometres on two wheels, I've come to understand something profound: passion and purpose are more than abstract, lofty ideals. They're the fuel that keeps us going when the road is long and the sky turns dark.

Purpose gives your life direction. Passion gives it *fire*.

Some people live accidentally, without ever pausing to ask where they're headed – or why they're headed there. Others search tirelessly for purpose as if it were a buried treasure waiting to be discovered in a career, a cause or a calling.

I've come to believe something different. Purpose isn't something you find. It's something you shape.

And often, it's shaped in motion.

This chapter is about that fuel: what it is, why it matters, and how you can live more of your life with your hands on the handlebars of something that truly matters to you.

Purpose and motorcycling

There's something about riding a motorcycle that strips life back to its essence. The wind, the road and the thrum of the engine pull you into the now. It's no surprise that many riders say they feel most alive when they're in the saddle. The Zen masters spoke of this quality as *being in the moment*, free of thought and ego, where action occurs without effort. As we've already seen in Chapter five, we now call it *flow*. On a long ride, especially through winding hills or open country, you don't just find flow: you *become* it.

In that state, deeper questions surface. Riding, like life, doesn't offer guarantees or complete control. The Stoics knew this well (about life, not motorcycling). They taught that we must distinguish between what we can control – our actions, choices and attitudes – and what we cannot (the weather, the traffic, the twists and turns of fate). Purpose, in this sense, isn't about chasing certainty or success. It's choosing how you respond to the road beneath your wheels. It's the rider riding calmly in a storm, hand steady on the throttle.

Over time, the ride becomes a metaphor for living with intention and purpose. Just as a finely tuned bike responds instantly to the smallest input, a purposeful life moves with clarity and grace. You begin to notice synchronicities, meaningful coincidences that seem to guide you, and trust that you're on the right track. You don't find purpose once and keep it forever. You ride into it again and again, with curiosity, courage and commitment. And like a good ride, it's less about the destination, and more about the way you show up for the journey.

As the Stoics taught, purpose isn't about grand outcomes: it's how you live today. Marcus Aurelius wrote, "At dawn, when you have trouble getting out of bed, tell yourself: I have to go to work as a human being." Your work, your ride, your life. You're ticking boxes. You're showing up with presence, courage and alignment.

The Stoics didn't chase applause. They pursued a quiet, steady kind of purpose: to live honourably and true to their nature.

That's a ride worth taking.

The ride to autonomy, competence and connection

An important finding of the research by Deci and Ryan was that people who undertook activities based on intrinsic motivation found those activities interesting and pleasant, and also that three basic psychological drivers were met: the desires for autonomy, competence and relatedness. Motorcycling is one of the few activities I've found that naturally delivers all three. Let's look at these three drivers:

- *Autonomy*. This is the right to be self-governing or self-ruling; to be the ruler of your own destiny, and the sense that you have at least some control over your life. You're motivated by choice. On the bike, you decide your route, your pace and your rest stops. You plan the ride and weather is not going to stop you. There's a freedom in that which no other vehicle or activity can match – but then again, I'm very biased.

- *Competence*: People need and want to develop, expand and build on their skills. They want to raise their capabilities to the level of mastery. This need to get better at what one does, to constantly improve, is reinforced by the release of dopamine in the brain, which, through a virtuous cycle, increases drive and intrinsic motivation. Every ride improves your skills – your ability to corner smoothly, brake predictably, read road conditions, and make quick decisions. With every passing kilometre, you build to mastery.

- *Connection*: We are social creatures. We need connection and caring. We need to know we belong and are accepted by our tribe, and we like to care for other people. As author Seth Godin says, "We all need to belong to a tribe of like-minded people." There's a bond among riders, often exhibited by a wave from a stranger in the opposite lane, shared nods at a servo, or a quiet chat over coffee after a hard ride. It's subtle but real.

You don't need a bike to feel those things, of course. But if you've ever ridden, you'll know how naturally those things are.

Merging autonomy, competence and connection with passion and purpose

The two-year study conducted by the Center for Healthy Minds and the University of Wisconsin-Madison, 'Purpose in life predicts better emotional recovery from negative stimuli' found that having a purpose in life alters the brain positively. Changes in brain chemistry – especially increases in dopamine (the feel-good neurotransmitter produced by the brain as a reward for particular types of behaviour that insured the survival of the species) and changes in the amygdala – decrease stress and build resilience. Their work also highlights that having a purpose alters the way the brain filters incoming messages. It also seems that having a purpose in life reduces your chances of having a stroke or heart attack or developing dementia.

Having a purpose in life motivates you. It promotes autonomy, because you must move towards it yourself. It builds competence, since progress demands the development of new skills. And it fosters connectedness, because for most of us, purpose can only be fulfilled in relationship with others. In fact, a clear sense of purpose not only guides you but also inspires and attracts others to your cause. One strength builds on the next, creating a foundation on which the rest of life is constructed.

I've ridden solo many times across long stretches of straight road that went for hundreds of kilometres. Hours at a time, passing no one. Just the thrumming of the engine, the wind pressing against my body, and the endless ribbon of road stretching to the horizon. Yet when I did see another rider, or even a truckie, the wave or nod that we exchanged carried a surprising warmth. Out there, autonomy is absolute. Competence is essential. And even in solitude, connection will appear – in small, human gestures that say, "You're not alone out here."

From interest to identity

When I was six years old, I would regularly stand outside our family's milk bar in Sydney and gaze in wonder across the street at the motorbikes parked outside the pub. They were mostly Triumphs and BSAs, loud and powerful and, at least to a young boy, thrillingly dangerous. I was captivated and fascinated by both the bikes and the people.

My six-year-old mind asked questions: Why do people act the way they do? What makes one person happy and another not so happy? What does it all mean?

Decades later, I would realise that those early loves – motorcycles and human psychology – weren't just childhood curiosities. They were breadcrumbs, hints pointing me towards something deeper. A vocation. Over the years, those interests matured and became a large part of my life and identity. I wasn't just a bloke who liked riding or one who read self-development and psychology books. I became a rider. A coach. A teacher. A guide.

We all walk that journey, from curiosity to calling, in some way. It begins with paying attention to what lights you up, what draws you in, what never quite lets you go. It continues as you experiment, explore and refine. And if you're lucky, it ends in a life that feels deeply your own.

Purpose isn't found. It's discovered

People will often ask me how they can find their purpose. But that's the wrong question. Purpose isn't discovered, like a lost set of keys. It's *un*covered, something hidden beneath the surface of your daily life. You can't manufacture it; it evolves and flows through you when you get out of your own way. To let this happen, you need to silence Crocky and other internal negative mind chatter. Life will present opportunities to you to let go and grow. And, if you remain open, your purpose will reveal itself so clearly that you will not be able to ignore it.

Want to uncover your purpose?

Your purpose will reveal itself through *action*, *reflection* and *honest listening* to your reactions, your longings and even your discomfort. Here are ten useful questions to ask yourself to uncover your purpose:

1. When I think about the future, what excites me?

2. What activities or experiences make me feel most alive?

3. If I could leave a legacy, what would I most want to be remembered for?

4. What challenges and struggles have I faced, and what have I learnt from them?

5. How can I combine my natural abilities with my passions to serve others or contribute to a greater cause?

6. Whom do I admire, and why?

7. What impact do I want to have on the people around me, and how can I use my unique strengths to help them?

8. What accomplishments or achievements am I most proud of? Why?

9. If I could do one thing for the rest of my life, what would it be?

10. Beyond external success, what does my soul long for, and how can I honour that desire?

This process of uncovering your purpose is something that the visionary architect and systems thinker R. Buckminster Fuller knew intimately. Fuller, who was often called "the world's friendly genius," had a moment of profound transformation in 1927. On the verge of suicide, feeling like a failure by society's standards, he stood on the shores of Lake Michigan and asked himself a life-altering question: "What is it I can do, that no one else can do, in the way that I can do it?" From that moment, he resolved to live not by conventional measures of success but by doing what he believed was the right thing, correcting course when needed, and trusting he would be supported if he was truly "on track". Time and again, he found that support appeared, often coincidentally, and often just in the nick of time.

Fuller believed that nature had a hidden design for everything and that if we align with it and follow our unique path, we will not only achieve our goals but also grow into the kind of person into which those goals were meant to shape us. The goal, whether a new car or a new idea, is almost secondary to the growth it demands.

For me, motorcycling has always offered a similar mirror. On a long solo ride, there's nowhere to hide from myself. There's just the bike, the road and my thoughts. The silence clarifies. The rhythm strips away the noise. And what remains are often whispers of purpose – small but insistent signals that say, "Pay attention to this."

That's what living with purpose often feels like. Not thunderous clarity, but a quiet knowing. Not a polished mission statement, but a nudge towards what matters.

Like Fuller, I've found that when I follow those nudges, when I stay on track with what feels deeply right, even if I don't yet see the full map, life tends to offer support in surprising ways. It's as if the road, both literal and metaphorical, responds when I'm heading in the right direction.

The hero's journey (and 'bliss' misunderstood)

Joseph Campbell, the scholar who mapped the mythic structure behind many of the world's stories, famously said, "Follow your bliss." The phrase has been both embraced and misunderstood. Some people assume it means "do what feels good" or "only do what brings joy", but Campbell clarified that bliss was a sense of deep alignment and the feeling that you're doing what you're here to do, even when it's hard.

I've had moments on the road like that. Once, while riding through the

Victorian Alps, I hit a sudden hailstorm. There was nowhere to pull over, no shelter, and the ice pelted my visor like bullets. It wasn't blissful in the usual sense, but something inside me was utterly *alive*. Every nerve lit up. Every choice mattered. I was *present*. That, too, is bliss.

Bliss doesn't mean comfort. It means congruence.

Campbell's broader insight, the "Hero's Journey", is equally important. He described a pattern of storytelling across cultures where the hero:

- Leaves the known world
- Faces trials and challenges
- Encounters mentors and allies
- Gains insight or a gift
- And returns transformed.

That describes every motorcycle tour I've ever done. You leave comfort. You face weather, fatigue, doubts. You meet unexpected guides in the forms of friendly strangers, wise locals, and even parts of yourself. And if you persist, you come home changed.

The Hero's Journey isn't a fantasy. It's a framework for living with purpose. The road teaches it, again and again.

The purpose-driven life isn't always glamorous

Let's be honest. "Purpose" gets romanticised. As if once you find it, you'll live happily ever after, like in a fairytale. The false promise is that after you find your purpose, life becomes one smooth, inspired ride. It doesn't. Carrying emotional baggage, as we all do, blocks the natural flow of life and energy through our clinging to past experiences, fears or identities. Passion and purpose arise not from clinging but from *clearing the way*. From letting go.

Living with purpose doesn't always look graceful. Sometimes life asks you to participate when you're exhausted, confused or disheartened. Sometimes you'll question your direction. Sometimes other people will. But purpose is like the heavy keel of a yacht that provides stability at all times and allows the yacht to resist crosswinds without tipping over or being pushed off track. It reminds you why you keep going when the weather turns or the path is unclear. One of Nietzsche's oft-repeated sentences, from his 1899 book *Götzen-Dämmerung* (*Twilight of the Idols*), was "He who has a why to live can bear almost any how." Your purpose provides you with a huge why!

Over the years, I've coached thousands of people, from executives to young adults to retirees, regarding their purpose. For some, it arrived like a bolt of lightning. For most, it was more like learning to ride a bike: at first, it was awkward, uncertain, full of wobbles and doubts, but then it all came together. And off they went.

Some think their purpose is their job. Or their relationship. Or some perfect "calling". But what we often discovered together was that purpose often hides in plain sight: in what angers us, what absorbs us, what moves us to act.

You don't need a business card with the word "purpose" on it. Rather, you need a life that *feels aligned* with your values and what you think is the right way to act. Sometimes that's expressed in a career. Sometimes in parenting, or writing, or volunteering. Sometimes it's how you ride through your days with kindness, curiosity or courage.

As Viktor Frankl once wrote, 'Life is never made unbearable by circumstances, but only by lack of meaning and purpose." Purpose doesn't erase pain. It makes it bearable. Sometimes it makes it transformative. And, as Winston Churchill once stated, "It's not enough to have lived. We should be determined to live for something."

Passion: The emotional throttle

If purpose is your compass, then passion is your throttle. Passion gives your life colour, intensity and momentum. It helps you ride through storms because you care enough to keep going. I've ridden through bone-soaking rain, blistering desert heat and exhaustion so deep it made me question my sanity. But I never gave up because something deeper was pulling me forward. Passion.

It doesn't always roar. Sometimes it's a whisper or a subtle nudge. But other times, it's a fierce fire that propels you through doubt or pain. We often associate passion with excitement, but it's more than that. It's energy directed towards something meaningful. Passion gives you the grit to persist and the resilience to get back up after you've fallen.

More than just making you feel alive, passion makes you a force. It gives you presence, magnetism and determination. Where others might quit, the passionate dig deeper. They remember why they started. They don't just ride; they ride with meaning.

The wake-up calls

Purpose and passion often become clearer in times of disruption, not when things are easy. Retirement was a wake-up call for me. After decades of meaningful work, suddenly the roles and routines disappeared.

But purpose doesn't retire. It adapts.

Retirement confirmed to me that my identity wasn't tied to a title or salary. It was tied to who I am. That is, someone who leads, teaches, and inspires. That didn't stop with the closing of an office door. It just moved onto new roads. This book is one of those roads.

Other wake-up calls came more abruptly by such things as a crash, a health scare, a relationship breakdown. Life has a way of sending messages, first as whispers, then as slaps, then as storms. A saying often attributed to Buckminster Fuller puts it like this:

> When you're off track, Great Spirit (he loved the American Indian traditions) will give you a tap on the shoulder. If you don't get the mes-

sage, you get a bigger tap. If you don't get the message, you get a slap on the back. And if you still don't get the message, you get run over by a Mack truck!

The question isn't "Will these moments come?" It's "How will you respond to them when they do?"

Experiencing a motorcycle crash will often force a rider to stop, slow down and re-evaluate. Other times it will be something more subtle, perhaps a persistent restlessness or a quiet sense that they're living someone else's script. These moments can be terrifying, but they're also clarifying. They shake us awake, urging us to confront what lies beneath the surfaces of our daily lives. And, as has often been attributed to Carl Jung, "Until you make the unconscious conscious, it will direct your life and you will call it fate."

Wake-up calls are invitations to consciousness. They almost always point you back to purpose.

When purpose evolves

There's a myth that purpose is static. A single, unchanging mission that you commit to for life. But in truth, purpose evolves as you do.

In my twenties, my purpose was about learning – absorbing everything I could about psychology and self-development. And riding. In my thirties and forties, it became about contribution, coaching, teaching, and guiding others to live more fully. In my fifties and sixties, it shifted again, towards reflection, writing and legacy.

I've just turned seventy, and purpose still pulses strong. But it's less about striving and more about being. Less about proving, and more about presence.

You don't have to have it all figured out. You just need to keep listening. Keep watching environmental feedback and adjusting. Keep refining. Keep moving in the direction that feels right for you.

My current purpose?

To inspire and motivate myself and others to unlock and live more of our true potential.

It's simple. It's portable. And it aligns with who I am, whether I'm writing a book, coaching a client, riding with a mate, being with my family or speaking to a stranger in a roadside café.

Precession: Purpose and the power of indirect impact

Buckminster Fuller's concept of precession suggests that our true purpose will often reveal itself indirectly, as a side effect of pursuing our goals. In astronomy, precession refers to a change in the axis of rotation of a planet, similar to the wobble of a spinning top, although in the case of Earth, one "wobble" takes 26,000 years. Fuller's concept of precession extended beyond physics and astronomy:

> Precession is the effect of bodies in motion on other bodies in motion. … The effect of the sun on the earth, the gravitational pull, is to make the earth go into orbit around the sun, at 90 degrees not at 180 degrees. So, the pull is 180 degrees, the resultant is 90 degrees, and this is precession. I find this is one of the notions that man is not really used to, he really thinks about his 180 degrees, and he expects 180 degrees all the time, not realizing this other angle, the resultant, precession.

In other words, whenever something is moving towards a goal, there are other effects that occur as byproducts.

In simple terms, precession is the idea that when we aim for a specific goal, the most significant outcomes may occur at ninety degrees to our original direction. These are unintended, yet crucial effects.

Fuller provided a bee as an example. A bee's goal is to collect nectar to take back to the hive. However, in the process of collecting nectar, the unintentional side effect is that it pollinates flowers as it goes, thus enabling new life to grow. Although the bee's true purpose is to simply nourish the colony, it also sustains the ecosystem. Similarly, in life, pursuing a goal with passion often leads to unanticipated rewards that shape our legacy and impact, albeit they are things that we may never have planned.

This is precession in action: the unintended positive effects of chasing our goals can turn out to be our true contribution. For example, pursuing a career for the simple goal of financial success may lead to opportunities to inspire others, build relationships or influence wider communities in ways you never expected. These precessional effects – unintended side outcomes, the unexpected ripple effects of pursuing what matters most to you – are often nature's *true purpose*.

Living your purpose daily

You don't need to quit your job, sell all your belongings, live in an ashram or ride a motorcycle across the country to live with purpose and passion. You just need to bring more *you* to what you do. You need to infuse your days with more intention, more alignment and more truth.

Ask yourself:

- What makes me feel alive?
- What brings me peace?
- What do I love so much I'd do it for free?
- What am I passionate about?

And then, how can you bring *more* of that into your life? Even in small ways?

Maybe it's one passionate conversation per day. One hour a week doing the thing that makes your heart beat faster. One decision that moves you closer to who you really are.

Living with purpose doesn't require perfection. It requires presence. It means being awake to your choices, alert to your inner compass, and willing to course-correct when you drift.

You will drift. That's life. The goal isn't to ride straight forever. It's to notice when you're off track and turn back with compassion and clarity.

The power of Ikigai

One of the most useful models I've found for aligning purpose and passion is the Japanese concept of *Ikigai* ("reason for being"). Héctor García and Francesc Miralles portrayed this concept beautifully in their best-selling book *Ikigai: The Japanese Secret to a Long and Happy Life*. It is often visualised as the intersection of four circles:

1. What you love

2. What you're good at

3. What the world needs

4. What you can be paid for.

At the centre is your ikigai. Your sweet spot. Your unique blend of passion, talent, service and sustainability. It is illustrated in the following image:

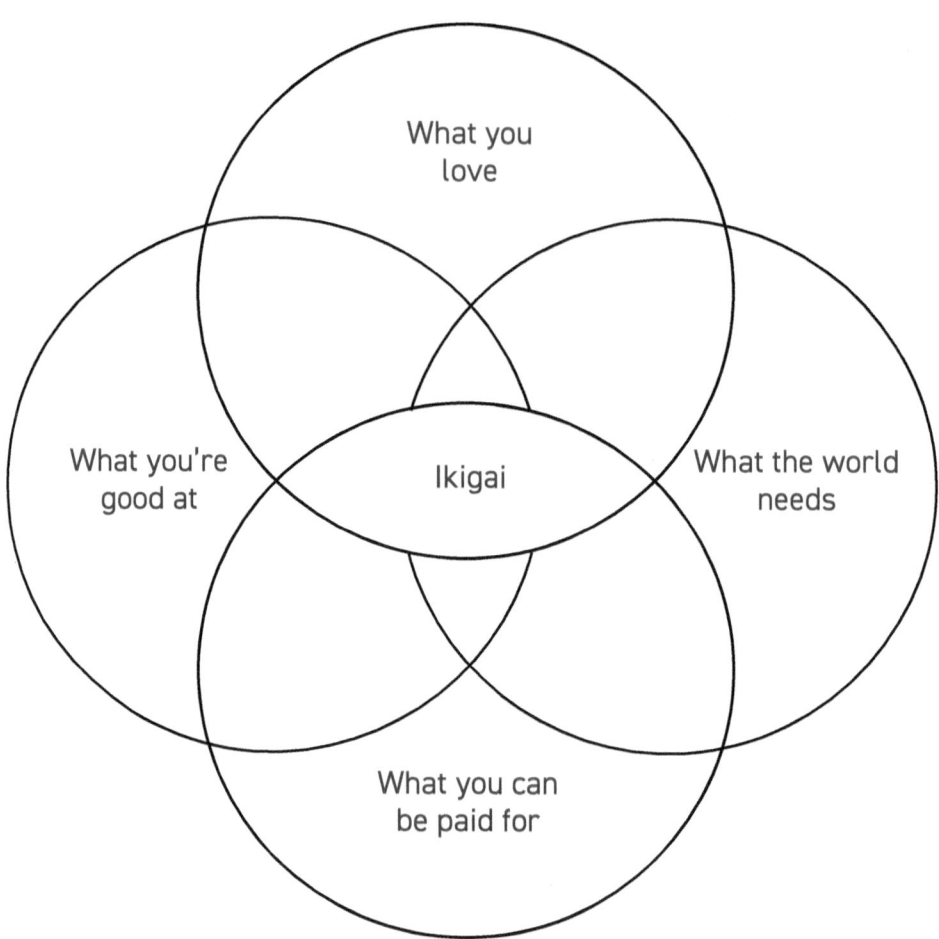

You might not overlap all four circles perfectly. That's okay. Even aligning three of them can give you a powerful sense of purpose.

For many riders, motorcycling hits all the emotional and psychological sweet spots, even if it doesn't pay the bills. That's still valid. Not everything meaningful has to be monetised. Some things are just for the soul.

Try sketching your own ikigai. Write down your answers to the four circles. Then look for overlaps. You might be surprised at what emerges. Or what's been there all along.

Purpose and passion in the saddle

Let me leave you with a few final motorcycle moments that illustrate what purpose and passion look like in action.

- *The broken chain in outback SA*: Many years ago, while riding a Honda 750/4, I broke a chain hundreds of kilometres from help. Rather than panic, I laughed. The South Australian outback was hot that day: it was forty degrees. I was sweating and stranded. But I felt oddly peaceful. Because I was *where I belonged*, on the road, in the moment, in the flow. That's passion. (And, luckily, before too long, a truck came by and rescued me.)

- *The coaching call before a ride*: Sometimes I would make coaching calls just before hitting the road. It always amazed me how the energy of helping someone would flow into my ride. My throttle hand felt lighter, my eyes clearer. That's alignment.

- *Riding with my mate Ian*: We've clocked a couple of hundred thousand kilometres together. And every ride is more than a trip. It's mateship. It's conversations about life. About meaning. About the road ahead – literally and figuratively. That's connection.

Purpose isn't one big thing. It's thousands of little things. It's who you are when no one's watching. It's how you treat others, how you respond to challenge, how you follow your inner voice – even when it whispers something inconvenient.

Passion isn't always fireworks. It's often the low, steady hum that keeps you going. The love that doesn't need words. The commitment that doesn't need applause.

Together, they form the engine of a meaningful life.

The road ahead

In the end, this book isn't just about motorcycles. It's about the open road *within*. The one we each ride every day, through decisions, relationships and challenges.

To ride that road with purpose is to live fully. To ride it with passion is to love fiercely.

So, here's my invitation:

- Choose the roads that matter.

- Ride towards what lights you up.

- Face obstacles, fears and doubts head on and with courage.

- Don't wait for a crisis to ask yourself what your life is for.

- And when in doubt, throttle on, because moving creates side effects which could just possibly be the main effect!

Because none of us are here to sleepwalk through life. You are not here to tick boxes and follow maps drawn by others. You are here to *ride your own ride*. To live with clarity, courage and joy.

That's what this road has taught me. That's what I now pass on to you.

Live with purpose. Ride with passion. And never stop exploring the road within.

Chapter 10

THE ART OF THE LONG RIDE: ENDURANCE AND PATIENCE

Long-distance riding over days, weeks or months is more than just an adventure; it's a melting pot for character development. Long days in the saddle create a kind of rhythm that only reveals itself when the mind quietens, the body settles and the road becomes your companion rather than your adversary. In these moments, motorcycling transcends mere transportation and becomes a journey inward as much as a journey on the road.

The world's toughest riders: The Iron Butt Association

For some, long-distance motorcycling becomes more of a way of life than merely a personal challenge. The Iron Butt Association (IBA), which proudly refers to itself on its logo as "The World's Toughest Riders", is a global community of motorcyclists dedicated to endurance riding. Their motto? The World is Our Playground. IBA-certified rides range from the iconic SaddleSore 1000 (1,000 miles in under 24 hours) to the astonishing Bun Burner Gold (1,500 miles in 24 hours) and even multi-day, continent-spanning marathons like the Iron Butt Rally, an 11-day ride covering up to 11,000 miles. For all long-distance rides, strategy, endurance and grit trump horsepower and speed every time.

Why do they do it, and what you, motorcyclist or not, can learn from it

Iron Butt riders do these things to test themselves and prove that the impossible is possible. The badge is not just for bragging rights. It's a symbol of the mental grit and physical fortitude that they had to exhibit to earn the badge. And, as with all great rides, it's less about speed and more about resilience, patience and tenacity. My questions to you – whether motorcyclist or not: When did you last really test yourself? When was the last time you went even a little bit beyond the limits you thought you had? When did you last do/accomplish/achieve what you and those around you had thought was impossible? How far have you slipped into mediocrity and comfort? Is it time for you to challenge yourself?

Over the years, I've ridden my fair share of long days in the saddle, many over 1,000 kilometres (but not IBA rides, though). I've also been on the road for weeks and months at a time, so I know there's a lot that can be learnt about riding and life through such trips. Every rider begins with a destination in mind, but the real arrival happens much closer to home: inside your own heart and mind.

A long-distance motorcycle tour teaches you lessons no classroom ever could

Long days in the saddle shape your character as much as they condition your riding skills. A long ride will show you not only the landscape but also the very essence of who you are. As the kilometres pass, new layers of self are revealed, including the dark parts you avoid (the shadow) and strengths you didn't know you had. Riders across the world tell the same story. The bike doesn't just take you places. It transforms you. It helps you to make peace with uncertainty. Every storm, every breakdown, every wrong turn and every set of twisties, all of it is shaping you into a stronger and wiser version of yourself.

The road shapes the rider

Motorcycling has a way of quietly but powerfully reshaping who you are. This is evident in the stories of modern-day solo adventurers like Noraly

The Art Of The Long Ride: Endurance and Patience

Schoenmaker (Itchy Boots) and Kinga Tanajewska (On Her Bike). Both women remind us that the road reveals more than just the world; it reveals the rider, as well. Both bikers have criss-crossed continents solo, facing everything from mechanical failures and difficult borders to extreme weather and deep isolation. Schoenmaker says, "Riding solo isn't about being fearless. It's about doing it anyway, fear and all." Both women have become YouTube stars. Their YouTube channels are highly successful: Itchy Boots has about three million followers, and On Her Bike has several hundred thousand followers.

Schoenmaker often speaks about how solo motorcycling has taught her to let go of rigid expectations and embrace uncertainty. When plans fall apart – and they often do – she's learned to see those detours not as failures but unexpected invitations to grow, to see new places and meet new people. Each unplanned border crossing, flooded road, or breakdown in a remote village builds self-reliance and mental flexibility. As Schoenmaker puts it, "You learn that the world doesn't work the way you want it to, and that's okay."

Tanajewska, too, reflects on how long-distance motorcycling reshaped her self-image and helped her develop inner strength. As a woman, setting out alone taught her not only courage but deep trust, not only in herself and her instincts but also in the goodness of strangers. She has learnt that "the world is not as dangerous as it seems." The shift from fear-based thinking to open-minded curiosity doesn't happen overnight. Rather, the shift occurs "mile after mile", and it shapes your character in ways no classroom or self-help book ever could.

Both women highlight something many riders (including me) have discovered: the longer you spend in the saddle, especially alone, the more you develop habits that carry over into everyday life. You become more patient, more accepting of things outside your control, and more present in the moment. And, perhaps most importantly, you begin to understand that challenges are not obstacles designed to stop you. Rather, they are experiences that can shape you and help you grow.

The paradox of control

A paradox emerges on a long ride: the more you try to control everything, the more you realise how little control you actually have. The weather changes. Plans fall apart. Bikes break down. Detours appear, unannounced. Yet in accepting this lack of control, you find freedom. You can only control the controllables: your attitude, your choices, your reactions.

Epictetus reminds us, "The chief task in life is simply this: to identify and separate matters so that I can say clearly to myself which are externals not under my control, and which have to do with the choices I actually control."

The open road is the perfect place to practise this ancient wisdom.

Each "obstacle" provides an invitation to grow, adapt and become the kind of person who is shaped by the journey rather than merely enduring it.

Other real-world lessons from the saddle

Take Steph Jeavons, for example, the British rider who circled the globe solo, riding across all seven continents on her Honda CRF250L. Along the way, she faced deep loneliness, breakdowns in desolate landscapes and bureaucratic brick walls. But each challenge, as she later shared, peeled away layers of self-doubt and replaced them with calm confidence and a wider perspective. The road taught her to value solitude as a place where real self-understanding begins.

Elspeth Beard, another British rider, was one of the first women to ride solo around the world. This was in the early 1980s. Back then, a lone woman on a motorcycle (it was a BMW R60/6) was a rare and radical sight. Having faced everything from bike crashes to corruption at borders, Elspeth credits her journey for not only making her more resourceful but also teaching her that limits are often illusions set by fear, not reality.

The Art Of The Long Ride: Endurance and Patience

Fear is often just imagination dressed as fact

Ted Simon was one of the first and best-known proponents of motorcycling as a path to personal growth. He first rode around the world in the 1970s on a Triumph Tiger 100. (He repeated the feat in the early 2000s.) Simon's first journey, which was recounted in the classic book *Jupiter's Travels*, was more about the stripping away of his assumptions than the sheer distance travelled. As he rode through deserts, jungles, war zones and remote villages, Simon realised that the world was both more dangerous and more generous than he had ever imagined. The trip taught him that fear is often just imagination dressed as fact and that real strength is born of vulnerability, from putting yourself in situations where you don't know what's coming next and learning to trust that you'll adapt.

Note Simon's phrase: *Fear is often just imagination dressed as fact.* I've been in many situations in out-of-the-way places where I had to rely on inner strength to keep going. I have also often found this to be the case with many of my coaching clients. When they did the things that they feared, they realised that their fears were largely fantasies fabricated by their minds (Hello, Crocky). When they "felt the fear and *became* it anyway", things usually turned out okay. And often far better than okay.

Simon wrote that his biggest transformation was internal. By the time he returned home, he no longer saw the world in terms of borders, status or politics. Rather, he saw it through the lens of human connection and personal responsibility. In his words, "I used to think the world was full of strangers. Now I know it's full of friends I haven't met yet." His story is a clear reminder that the journey changes the rider far more deeply than the miles ever could. "I set out looking for the world, but what I found was myself."

And of course, there are countless lesser-known riders whose stories never make YouTube or the news. Men and women who set out looking for freedom but also discover resilience and grit. Riders who learn to trust themselves when the GPS fails, who learn patience when stranded for hours, and who learn humility when nature reminds them how small they really are. Epictetus was on to something when he wrote in *The Discourses,* "We must make the best use that we can of the things that are in our power, and use the rest according to their nature." Every ride, every setback, every twist in the road is an invitation to focus on what we can do, our mindset, our pace, our reactions – and to let go of the rest. If you let it, the ride will shape your character, one kilometre at a time.

Ten defining traits and habits that are shaped by motorcycle touring

The following qualities shaped by the open road can be harnessed to tackle challenges both on and off the bike, demonstrating how motorcycle touring offers a path to deeper personal development and strength.

1. Self-reliance and personal responsibility

Long-distance riding is often a course in responsibility and self-reliance. You're on the open road, hundreds of kilometres from the next town. It's just you and your bike. Your choices and decisions will determine your experience. Bearing full responsibility for your decisions fosters independence and sharpens judgement. If you take a wrong turn or break down, there is no one else to blame. Although it can be difficult and demanding at times, the long ride deepens your self-trust and builds self-confidence and a proactive, "can-do" mindset.

2. Grit and tenacity

Touring riders know that comfort is temporary, but the satisfaction of pushing through fatigue, weather and mechanical hiccups is permanent. Grit is the ability to keep going when the easy choice would be to stop. Tenacity and grit are the fuel that carry a motorcyclist through the toughest stretches of a journey, long after excitement and energy have faded. It's the same in all areas of life.

The Art Of The Long Ride: Endurance and Patience

I remember battling relentless headwinds on a remote section in New Zealand's South Island. It was the kind of day where every kilometre felt like two thousand metres and the landmarks on the horizon never seemed to get closer. It was cold, very cold, even though it was January and supposed to be summer. Even if I had wanted to stop, there was no safe place. Fatigue crept in, doubts whispered through my helmet, but I had no option but to tighten my grip, take some deep breaths and keep going. It's not skill or luck that gets you through grinding stretches like that. You need sheer determination and a tenacious refusal to give in to discomfort or defeat. This grit – the ability to stay focused, push through adversity and keep moving forward – again and again – and ferocity (see point 7) are what separates those who reach their destination from those who turn back.

3. Patience, and remaining calm under pressure

As they say, "Shit happens!" Plans change. Roads close. The weather will surprise you, regularly. Your GPS will malfunction, and you'll get lost. The rider who masters patience learns to meet these hurdles with a calm head, adapting rather than resisting.

Ian and I were near Byron Bay in northern NSW. It was hot. Very hot. Many non-bikers think that cold weather is what bikers dread, but for Ian and me and many others, it's the heat. You can usually get warm with good gear like a heated vest and heated seats and grips, but even with a vented jacket and a cooling vest, 35-plus-degree heat is very hot and draining. On a backroad inland from Byron, we came across extensive roadworks controlled by traffic lights. We arrived just as the light turned red, so we were at the front of the line. There was not a skerrick of shade to be had, and the readout on my bike told me it was 38 degrees. There was a lot of activity –trucks laying gravel, water trucks dampening it down, and many workers.

We waited.

We thought it'd be just a couple of minutes.

We waited some more.

It was now 39 degrees. There we were, sitting in black jackets, boots and heavy motorcycle jeans in the blazing sun.

And we waited.

After ten very long minutes, we were baked.

The people in the cars behind us were probably also frustrated at how long it took to get that magic green light, but at least they were sitting in air-conditioned comfort.

Hot and flustered, after sixteen long minutes (yes, I was counting), we were able to move again, now dripping with sweat.

In moments like that – or, more correctly, sixteen minutes like that – patience, not frustration, saves the day.

Motorcycle touring runs on nature's timetable. You have no option but to accept setbacks. In life, it might be an illness, being made redundant, an accident, or a host of other unforeseen things. A seasoned rider learns early that fighting these moments with frustration only burns energy and clouds judgement. Instead, patience allows you to accept the pause, adjust your mindset and respond with calm. Whether it's waiting in the heat, waiting out an electrical storm under a safe shelter, or calmly addressing a mechanical hiccup by the roadside, patience keeps you grounded in the moment and helps you make more considered choices rather than impulsive ones.

4. Flexibility and adaptability

If long-distance touring teaches anything, it's flexibility and **adaptability**. On the road, plans can and will change, and successful riders learn to embrace it. Although I'm a planner, on longer, multi-week and multi-month rides, I've found that although I will start with a plan, the longer I'm away, the more flexible I need to be. Things change when you're on the road. You come across a washed-out bridge and are forced to take a massive detour.

Or you find unexpected highlights or meet interesting people that turn a quick break into a couple of hours. Sometimes, letting go of schedules leads to richer experiences.

The last three times we have ridden through Griffith, NSW, our GPS has led us astray in different ways. The last time, it took us to a very narrow gravel road. Neither of us is a fan of riding on gravel. As usual, we were on laden BMW road bikes. After about 250 metres of gravel, we stopped to reassess, as all that we could see stretching forever before us was more gravel. We had, somehow, also become seriously disorientated. A couple of minutes later, a massive truck came from the other direction, spraying dust and stones everywhere. It was huge. We wondered why it was on such a backroad. But there it was, heading towards us. There was barely enough room for the truck to pass us. We stood next to our bikes to steady them as it rumbled past, leaving us covered in dust. We then helped each other turn our bikes around on foot and then headed back to the sealed road, where we got out our trusty paper maps to work out which way to go.

Flexibility was vital that day. Being adaptable to changing circumstances is what transforms a setback into part of the adventure. Motorcycling teaches this lesson vividly: the road rarely unfolds exactly as imagined, but by staying flexible and open-minded, you can discover new paths and often richer experiences than the ones you had originally planned.

5. Humility: Acknowledging that the road is bigger than you

I was a young man, full of confidence, and I thought I could handle anything the road could throw at me when I did my first solo long ride from Sydney to Mossman Gorge in northern Queensland (about 6,000 kilometres there and back via the meandering route I took). The day started clear and calm. It was the kind of morning that makes you believe the world is on your side. But as the hours passed and the miles stretched out, the weather turned. A strong crosswind began hammering me, each gust a sharp reminder of just how small and insignificant I really was. Every bend demanded total focus. Every open stretch became a test of endurance. I gripped the bars tighter, but the harder I fought, the more the road seemed to push back. By the time I pulled my little Honda CB500/4 into a roadside stop, I was exhausted and humbled. The lesson was clear. The road doesn't bend to your will. It's bigger than you, and it always will be.

Motorcycling has a way of stripping away the ego. On the road, you're not the master of your surroundings; you're only a tiny part of them. The road, the weather, the machine and your own skill all play their part, but just your skill on the bike won't give you control. You learn to respect the conditions and adapt to them, but the most important thing to learn is to accept them.

That's humility. Understanding your place in a world that moves on with or without you. Accepting that what is, is – even if you don't like it. You're not the centre of the journey. You're just a traveller passing through.

This same lesson spills into life off the bike. The world isn't here to accommodate your plans, and life's twists and turns rarely unfold the way you expect or want them to. The sooner you accept that, the happier you'll be. The road teaches you to replace arrogance with attentiveness, impatience with presence, and control with acceptance. The road was there before you. It will be there long after you've gone. Your role is not to conquer it. Your role is to ride it well, with humility and grace.

6. Appreciation for the journey: The destination is merely an excuse for the ride

I learnt early in my motorcycling life that the real magic wasn't to be found at the destination. At first it was, of course. Like most new riders, I'd plan a trip with the goal firmly in mind. I'd map it and ride it as if it were a mission to be completed. But over time, something shifted. I started noticing the in-between.

One morning on a solo trip through western NSW, after camping the night at Gulgong, I rose to the soft light of dawn. The road stretched out like a lazy ribbon across the hills. Kangaroos watched me pack up, and the thick scent of eucalyptus hung in the air. It wasn't a particularly special day, but not long after I left, something clicked. This – the rumble of the engine, the wind tugging at my jacket, the slightly misty fresh air on my face and filling my lungs, the landscape slowly revealing itself turn by turn – *this* was the reason I rode.

And it still is.

Motorcycling teaches you that the journey is the goal. Rather than always striving for the next thing, the next goal, riding helps you to be present in the moment and enjoy the ride. To appreciate the journey for its own sake. The destination gives you direction, but riding the road gives you meaning.

7. The habit of ferocity

Steven Kotler, author and peak performance expert, refers to "ferocity" as the ability to rise *automatically and repeatedly* to any challenge – not just once but again and again, even when you're exhausted, uncertain or running on empty. To Kotler, ferocity doesn't mean being aggressive or reckless. Rather, "it's about relentless intention."

Ferocity is more than a mindset. It's a way of being that blends fierce and ongoing determination with unwavering focus. It involves committing yourself to a goal and pushing forward, no matter how difficult or uncomfortable the circumstances. It's the quiet strength to continue when others might quit, driven not by external circumstances but by your inner purpose.

When Kotler studied peak performers in sports and other areas of life, he found that what sets the highest achievers apart is their ability, over and over again, to apply intense focus, dedication and relentless drive to their goals. It's that phrase – "over and over again" – that really defines ferocity. Don't wait for inspiration or perfect conditions. Show up time after time, even when you're tired or things aren't going smoothly.

Ferocity, Kotler explains, is tied to the science of peak performance, the powerful mix of passion, purpose and persistence that trains your body and mind to push through fatigue, doubt and obstacles. Not brute force or stubbornness, but disciplined intensity that is practiced repeatedly until it becomes second nature.

Developing ferocity can be transformative by helping you develop the confidence, self-reliance and resilience to achieve ambitious goals that currently seem just beyond your reach. For example, if you plan to ride 1,400 kilometres in a single day but your longest ride so far has been 400 kilometres, the challenge will be as much mental as physical. Your focus needs to shift from speed to endurance, from simply finishing to finishing well – even if exhausted. You must stay sharp, and you have to adapt to the conditions, manage your energy and stay mentally tethered to your purpose.

Let's say you're on a long touring ride, and you're nearing the end of a 10-hour day. You started before sunrise, and now the sun is setting, your legs are stiff and you've got a couple more hours to go. The temptation to stop early is strong, but you remember your goal – and that's when ferocity kicks in. Stopping for a five-minute stretch break, you breathe deeply and remind yourself that pushing through this final stretch will not only get you closer to your destination but will also strengthen your resolve. The ride requires you to persist, stay focused, and overcome the discomfort, mile after mile after mile.

Ferocity isn't about winning races. It's about showing up again and again – fully, fiercely, no matter how long the road ahead.

8. Ride your own ride: Make your own choices

"Ride your own ride" is a well-worn saying among well, riders. It doesn't refer only to how you ride but also *what* you ride. Forget what's fashionable or has been hyped up by marketing. The best bike isn't the one that turns heads at the café. It's the one that fits you – your body, your riding style and the kind of journey you want to take.

In today's world of compulsive consumption, many people aspire to live the life of the rich and famous or at least to be seen in that light. Houses are bigger than ever, but families are getting smaller. Some people buy cars they can't afford so they can impress neighbours, colleagues and even strangers. We have more money to spend, yet personal debt is absurdly high. All this "stuff" is supposed to make us happy, but rates of anxiety and depression continue to climb.

This overconsumption mindset spills into the world of motorcycles. Big touring and adventure bikes with spaceship dashboards. Huge marketing campaigns whisper, "You need the biggest, baddest beast there is." But do you really need a 250-plus-kilogram motorcycle loaded with electronics, gadgets and horsepower just to explore the countryside or do a week-long tour? Maybe you do, but might you be caught up in the hype?

Ever heard of Emilio Scotto?

In 1985, after quitting his job in Buenos Aires, Emilio Scotto started what ended up being a ten-year ride around the world. He did it on a 1980 Honda Goldwing GL1100 Interstate. Not exactly the bike most people would choose for a round-the-world adventure, especially considering its size, weight and comfort features. At 350 kilograms, it's a big bike, built more for cruising American highways than navigating regions like the Amazon or the Sahara Desert. It was far from the conventional choice, but it worked for him. Comfort, reliability and familiarity mattered to Scotto more than convention or appearance. He chose the bike that fit his needs, not anyone else's. And I'm certain many people had opinions about his choice, because they always do!

This is one of the key traits that touring riders develop: the ability to choose what's right for them, not what's popular, expected, or conventional. It's a quiet self-trust, a willingness to follow their own compass. In life, we often face the temptation to select what looks right to others. The prestigious job with the fancy title, the socially approved partner, the lifestyle that earns applause. But the right "bike" for you may not look flashy or fit the accepted mould. It just needs to carry you well. It should feel natural, balanced and aligned with who you are and where you're going.

Choosing the right bike is a perfect metaphor for life. Reject the superficial allure of excess, reject the "affluenza" that feeds on comparisons and shallow desires. Forget about what's popular. What matters is that it works for you.

The Jeff Bezos framework for making decisions, blended with "10:10:10"

Amazon founder Jeff Bezos, who must have had to make tens of thousands of choices and decisions throughout his career and life so far, has developed a framework for deciding between different options. The framework splits decisions into two categories:

1. Type 1 decisions are the bigger decisions that require more time to think through. They have larger repercussions, some of which could be irreversible.

2. Type 2 decisions are reversible, so you can move faster in deciding them.

Most decisions are Type 2, but we will often overthink them and get stressed about them as a result.

To understand if a decision that you need to make is Type 1 or 2, ask yourself the questions summarised by "10:10:10": Will this decision matter in ten days from now? Ten months from now? Ten years from now? If your answer is yes to ten months and ten years, then you probably have on your hands a Type 1 decision that needs to be taken extra seriously.

9. Curiosity: A hunger for new places and experiences

Curiosity is the engine that pulls the motorcycle forward, not just across the physical landscape, but through the inner terrain of the mind, heart and spirit. Curiosity fuels the desire to leave the familiar behind and ask, "What's over that next hill?" or "What if I turned up *that* road instead of the one that I had planned?"

For the touring motorcyclist, curiosity is more than a personality trait. It's a way of life. It's the quiet, persistent hunger for the unfamiliar. It gets you out of bed in the morning and onto the bike, sometimes even with no clear destination in mind, because you're open to what might unfold if you trust the road.

When I first moved to New Zealand in August 1987, I had a map, a motorbike and a vague plan, and not much else. Pre-internet, pre–Google Maps, and pre–surfing the net for information. I found myself pointing the front wheel up roads I'd never heard of, with no idea what lay ahead. But time and time again, those spontaneous detours turned into the highlights of the ride. One day, I followed a winding backroad through rolling green countryside that eventually led me to the incredible art deco city of Napier on the east coast of the North Island. I'd never even heard of it before that ride, let alone how beautiful it was. But there it was, this unexpected gem, full of character, history and beauty. If I'd stuck rigidly to my original route, I'd have missed it completely.

That's the thing about curiosity: It's often accompanied by *flexibility*. The willingness to change your plans when something intriguing appears on the horizon. The understanding that detours are often where the gold is.

Curiosity changes how you experience the ride. It stops you from fixing your focus on getting somewhere fast. You start soaking in what's around you. The smells of wet forest or fresh-cut grass. The architecture of a forgotten rural town. The story behind a local pub's name. When you ride with curiosity, every kilometre is richer.

10. Control the controllables

One of the most important lessons we can learn is to focus on what we can control and accept what we cannot. This principle is central to Stoic philosophy. While we may not have control over external events, we always have control over our responses.

A powerful metaphor for this idea is the old Chinese story of the farmer and his horse. In the story, a farmer's horse runs away. His neighbours, seeing his misfortune, offer their sympathies. "How unlucky!" they say. But the farmer simply responds, "Maybe so, maybe not. We'll see." The next day, the horse returns, bringing with it a wild stallion. The neighbours, amazed, congratulate the farmer on his good fortune. "How lucky you are!" they exclaim. To which the farmer replies, "Maybe so, maybe not. We'll see."

The story continues as the farmer's son tries to tame the wild stallion, but in the process, he falls off and breaks his leg. The neighbours, again, offer their sympathy. "How unlucky!". And once more, the farmer responds, "Maybe so, maybe not. We'll see." A few days later, the country is at war, and the farmer's son is exempted from military service because of his broken leg. "How fortunate!" said his neighbours. The farmer's final reply is, "Maybe so, maybe not. We'll see."

That story illustrates beautifully the uncertainty of life. The farmer remains calm and accepting, not getting swept up in the immediate reactions of others. He focuses on what he can control: his own perspective and his response to the events unfolding. He doesn't let external circumstances dictate his sense of well-being. Instead, he holds space for the unpredictability of life, accepting that the full consequences of any situation aren't always immediately clear.

The same lesson applies when we're out on the road riding. When we hit a patch of bad weather or unexpected obstacles, our instinct may be to feel frustrated or upset. A sudden downpour on a long ride, for example, can feel like an unwelcome challenge, just like the farmer's lost horse. However, much like the farmer's calm acceptance of his situation, we have a choice in how we respond. We can grumble, curse the weather, and let it ruin the day. Or we can adjust our mindset, focus on what we can control – such as adjusting our speed, ensuring we're dressed for the conditions, and navigating carefully – and continue moving forward.

I remember a ride along the winding back roads of Caloundra on the Sunshine Coast of Queensland, heading towards a small town known for its incredible views. The forecast had promised a sunny day, but as I reached a more remote stretch of the route, the skies opened up. Rain fell in sheets, and visibility dropped dramatically. As the rain soaked through my jacket, I began to see riders in front of me pull over to the side, hoping to wait out the storm. There was no way of knowing how long it would last, but I knew I couldn't control that. So I kept moving.

Rather than getting frustrated or stressed, I took a moment to adjust my riding to the conditions. I eased off the throttle, increased my following distance and kept my eyes on the road, anticipating changes in the terrain. I couldn't control the weather, but I could control my pace, focus and reactions. The discomfort of being wet and cold was temporary, but my ability to stay composed and in control was within my power.

In that moment, the same principle that the farmer in the story had followed came into play. I wasn't going to fight the rain or get upset about the situation. Instead, I would adapt, focus on what I could control – my riding technique, my attitude and my preparation – and keep moving forward. The ride wasn't ideal, but it didn't have to be a negative experience. It was an opportunity to practice resilience, much like the farmer's stoic acceptance of life's ups and downs.

We must find strength in our ability to adjust to the road ahead, even when it's not what we expected. When we focus on controlling the controllables, we grow our resilience and reduce stress and frustration, in the process becoming better at handling the challenges life throws our way.

Every long ride is a metaphor for life

The road stretches out ahead, full of unknowns. You can prepare as best you can, but the real test will be how you respond to what you didn't anticipate.

The Open Road Within

In 2021, Ian and I met up in Broken Hill, NSW, with a plan to ride north to Lightning Ridge – a place we'd been before. It was meant to be a cruisy ride. We delayed our usual early start due to the number of emus and wild goats we'd seen on the roads the day before. A later start felt safer. We covered about 400 kilometres before pulling into a tiny roadhouse just before Cobar. It had just turned one o'clock, and we were ready for lunch. I know what the time was, because that was when my phone rang. It was Miranda, calling with urgent news. South Australia was going into a COVID lockdown at midnight. If I wasn't home by then, I'd be stuck out of the state indefinitely – maybe for weeks.

Suddenly, the day had changed.

This was an Epictetus moment, if ever there was one. *We cannot choose our external circumstances, but we can always choose how we respond to them.* And through that response, we become the person the road demands – one kilometre at a time.

Ian and I ate quickly, and then we said our goodbyes. He lives in New South Wales, so he wasn't affected. But there were 1,125 kilometres between me and home, and I'd already ridden over 400 kilometres, in the wrong direction, that morning. This was going to be a big day! I turned the bike around, rode the 400 kilometres back to Broken Hill, and then kept going into the night, through Peterborough, Burra, then Gumeracha until finally rolling into my driveway at Crafers West at 11:40 pm. Twenty minutes to spare! I'd done over 1,500 kilometres that day, and about a third of it was ridden in the dark of night through unfamiliar territory.

It took every trait that the long ride teaches to make that journey:

- Self-reliance and quick decision-making.
- Grit to push through fatigue.
- Patience and calm under time pressure.
- Flexibility and adaptability to change plans instantly.

The Art Of The Long Ride: Endurance and Patience

- Humility – riding carefully through the dark, knowing that a split-second lapse in attention if a kangaroo crossed the road in front of me could end the whole thing.

- Appreciation – for the moment, the freedom to ride, and arriving home safely.

- Ferocity – that relentless focus to keep going hour after hour.

- The whole day was an exercise in controlling the controllables.

- And, of course, having the right bike for the job. I was on a BMW R1250RT, which is designed for long-distance travel.

I don't normally ride at night out in the country. The risk of striking wildlife is just too high. But sometimes, life throws you a curveball. When it does, you will either rise to the moment or you won't.

That night, I rose to it. Not because I had to prove something, but because life demanded it.

The value of the long ride lies in how it shapes the rider within. It demands presence and teaches you that setbacks are temporary. That progress is measured not in leaps but in the steady, deliberate passage of mile after mile. That success is not measured by how few setbacks you experience, because the setbacks are part of the journey and one must learn to meet them with grace. The long ride teaches you to *refuse to give up*. To trust the process, and yourself. To take the highs and lows with equal poise, and to see the journey as the reward.

Motorcycle travel provides education for living. It changes you for the better. Forever. And isn't that, in the end, what life is all about?

Chapter 11

RIDING THE INVISIBLE ROAD: INTUITION, SYNCHRONICITY AND TRUST

There is a certain type of road that doesn't show up on any map. You can't GPS it and no one else can ride it for you.

The road I'm talking about here is an invisible road. It is one we navigate by feel, intuition, hunches, and with the aid of that subtle voice within (not Crocky) that quietly says, "Go this way."

This chapter is about the open road within.

On a motorcycle, the open road within becomes more than a metaphor. The longer you ride (and some would argue the longer you live), the more you sense that there are some things that logic and the rational mind can't explain. Night riding is a good example. You can only see as far as your headlight beam, yet you trust that the road continues beyond the light. Life is the same: we're rarely shown the full journey, but intuition gives us just enough light for the next bend.

You choose a road you weren't planning to take and "coincidentally" avoid a landslide; you stop just before an unpredicted storm hits; or you happen to meet a random stranger at a petrol station who says exactly what you needed to hear at that moment in your life. These events and experiences feel uncanny, almost orchestrated. Jung called it *synchronicity*: meaningful co-incidences that align with our inner journey and seem to be connected by a deeper, underlying pattern or purpose.

We'll explore how motorcycling sharpens our reflexes and our intuition;

how synchronicity can manifest; and how learning to let go of rigid plans can sometimes lead us to exactly where we need to be. If we trust the journey, not blindly but deeply, the open road within will become a mirror of who we are and also of the unseen forces that shape our path.

The inner compass: The quiet power of intuition

Intuition is often dismissed as vague, unreliable or unscientific. But the seasoned rider knows better. Sometimes the body knows, long before the conscious mind catches up. You sense the slickness of a patch of bitumen before you see it. You ease off the throttle before a blind corner reveals a stalled car. You pull over moments before a road train barrels past. You feel a tug to take a detour and later learn a serious crash occurred on your original route. Jung saw intuition as a key element in the process of self-discovery, guiding individuals towards greater personal growth and understanding.

These aren't guesses. They're not random. They're intuitive flashes, a form of inner knowing that arises before thought. Jung identified intuition as one of the four functions of consciousness, alongside thinking, feeling and sensing. For him, intuition wasn't mystical or magical. It is a valid way of perceiving reality that emerged from the unconscious. It taps into patterns, symbols and meanings before they reach conscious awareness.

Modern neuroscience backs this up. Beneath the level of awareness, the human brain is constantly processing. It "thin-slices", meaning that it makes rapid decisions based on experience in response to subtle environmental cues. This is how an experienced rider "just knows" something is off. The nervous system detects micro-signals faster than the conscious mind can articulate them.

Dopamine, the brain's motivator and mood regulator, also plays a role. When it is well regulated, dopamine produces that "click" of insight, the moment when something feels exactly right. But in excessive quantities, it can contribute to magical thinking or delusion.

Thus, intuition is grounded in deep perception, not fantasy.

Eugene Gendlin's 1978 book *Focusing* introduced a practice that I have used countless times myself and have taught to coaching clients. Gendlin describes focusing as tuning in to bodily sensations – referred to as the "felt sense" – to access deeper and often unconscious knowledge. An example of focusing and the felt sense might be when you leave home and have a nagging feeling that something is amiss. You go through a mental checklist. *Did I lock the door? Did I put the garbage out?* And then you think, *Did I leave the iron on?* and you feel a "click" inside. That's your body telling you what's wrong. And now you need to go home and switch the iron off!

Focusing pays attention to intuition felt in your body as a form of inner knowing that arises before thought, guiding individuals towards greater personal growth and understanding. Both concepts – intuition and focusing – highlight the importance of non-verbal, embodied awareness in perceiving and responding to subtle cues.

The Stoics didn't have a specific word for "intuition", but they spoke of alignment with nature and inner clarity. For instance, Epictetus constantly reminded us to act according to virtue, not just logic. Marcus Aurelius stated "Look within. Within is the fountain of good, and it will ever bubble up, if you will ever dig". Their message was simple: right action often stems from inner alignment rather than outer approval.

And the more we ride, the more we learn to listen. With enough road behind us, we become fluent in this quiet language of inner guidance.

One day when I followed my intuition

I've experienced things like this countless times, but one incident stands out. I was riding solo along the Great Ocean Road in Victoria. I was heading east towards Ian's place on the NSW South Coast. I was planning to follow the coast all the way there. The plan for today was simple: reach Wye River on the Great Ocean Road by sunset. But just past Lavers Hill, I began to feel uneasy. There was no obvious reason. The weather was fine. No roadworks. But I still had this strong internal nudge to stop.

I pulled over to study the map. An alternative route through the forest – a smaller, almost certainly narrower road – caught my eye. This was not part of the plan. But something in me said, "Take it." So, I did. And I was right; the road was certainly narrower – and very windy, with many 35 kph bends. But the surface wasn't dirt, which suited me. And it turned out to be one of the most memorable stretches of road on that entire two-week trip. Misty fern glades, no traffic, only the thrum of the engine – and the sense that I was exactly where I needed to be.

At breakfast the next morning, I found out that a landslide had closed the main road that I had originally planned to take.

Was it just pattern recognition? Or something more? Something deeper that led me to take that secondary road?

Modern spiritual teachers such as Deepak Chopra, Gabrielle Bernstein and Joe Dispenza would say intuition is the voice of a higher intelligence – Source, Spirit, or the quantum field. When your mind is quiet and your intentions are clear, you become receptive. For them, intuition is a download from the universe.

Whatever you call it – subconscious wisdom, embodied memory, cosmic signal – the value of intuition is undeniable. Especially on the road. The more in tune you are with your intuition, the more it tells you when to ride on and when to pause. It guides you to take the long way home and, sometimes, to find something you didn't even know you needed.

The real challenge isn't that intuition is rare. It's that we often ignore it.

One day when I didn't trust my intuition

It was the late 1970s. I was living in New South Wales. I had just returned from a four-month ride around half the country on my BMW R90S. (For non-bikers, this bike was the state of the art at that time. To this day, it remains one of the best bikes I've ever owned.) I was in my twenties, I owned one of the best bikes in the world, and I had a great job as a registered psychiatric nurse. And a wonderful girlfriend. I was loving life, and I felt invincible.

On a sunny spring morning, despite being hungover and tired from the night before, I insisted we go for a ride. My girlfriend didn't want to, and a loud inner voice was telling me not to go. But I ignored both.

We rode through the Blue Mountains, and at Mt Tomah on the Bells Line of Road, I did a tight right-hand 35 kph bend at over 100 kph. Unsurprisingly, I lost control. Everything went into slow motion. I slid down the road on my back. BANG! I hit the guardrail with my back. My girlfriend skidded down the centre line. The bike disintegrated in front of us. I can still remember vividly sliding down the road, heading for the guardrail; seeing my girlfriend slide down the road, also; and the bike doing cartwheels, with the tank and then the seat flying off, and then other bits and pieces flying skyward.

The ambulance officers had originally suspected that I had broken my back, but, luckily for me, I only sustained two broken ribs and some deep bruising. My girlfriend wasn't so lucky. She suffered deep cuts to her legs, and she had awful gravel rash and a very bruised body. To this day, she still has gravel in her knee. We were both admitted to Lithgow Hospital for three days, primarily to let my girlfriend rest and start to heal.

The bike was a write-off. It was uninsured, so I took a financial hit – though that was the least of my costs. As I've said numerous times, when things go wrong on a motorcycle, they can go very wrong very quickly.

That morning, intuition hadn't been a whisper. It had been a roar, a very strong voice inside me practically screaming, "Don't go out on the bike!" And I had ignored it. Ever since, when I have felt an inner alarm like the one I ignored that day, I have listened. Plus, my girlfriend hadn't wanted to go, but she had come because I was so insistent. I should have listened to her voice, too.

Riding The Invisible Road: Intuition, Synchronicity and Trust

The price of ignoring your intuition is often paid in flesh, metal or regret. Whichever lens you view it through – science, psychology, Stoic clarity or spiritual wisdom – intuition remains your inner compass. You're not predicting the future; you're recognising what your deeper self already knows.

Three lessons stuck with me from this accident:

- I wasn't invincible.
- Always get comprehensive insurance.
- Most importantly, always trust that inner voice.

When we listen, sometimes the road replies, not just with safety but also meaning. That's when intuition edges into something even more mysterious: synchronicity.

The Practice of Trusting Your Intuition

How do you develop trust in your intuition? Here are some rider-tested principles:

1. *Regularly create a space for stillness*: Ride in silence or spend at least fifteen minutes a day in solitude.

2. *Avoid rushing decisions*: Let the next step emerge naturally from a place of calm.

3. *Pay attention to patterns*: Notice moments when you "just know" something isn't right and pay attention to repeating messages or signs.

4. *Tune in to your body*: Often, heeding a gut feeling is wiser than overthinking. Learn to trust those embodied cues.

5. *Differentiate fear from intuition*: Fear contracts and creates panic; intuition is calm, clear and often accompanied by a sense of relief once followed.

Over time, your internal compass will become more accurate. Like a finely tuned bike, your intuitive system will begin to hum.

The science of synchronicity

Just as tuning in to your body helps refine your intuition, paying attention to synchronicities can further guide you on your journey. This principle is supported by both spiritual teachings and scientific research. As Deepak Chopra suggests, synchronicity increases when your life is aligned with your deeper self. Intentions act like tuning forks, aligning you with the right outcomes. Neuroscience backs this up. The brain's reticular activating system (RAS) filters sensory information based on what we focus on. Set a clear intention, and your brain begins to notice the relevant cues. Just like when you buy a red BMW R1300GS, you suddenly see them everywhere. On long tours I've noticed that once I set my mind on finding a country bakery, I suddenly "see" bakery signs everywhere. They ae always there but my attention wasn't tuned in to them. Likewise, when I've set the intention to ride safely, I seem to notice hazards earlier. Synchronicity isn't just cosmic magic; it's an alignment between focus and attention.

The Stoics understood this alignment, too. While they never used the term "synchronicity", their belief in *logos*, the rational order of the universe, echoes the idea that life is not random and that, rather, it unfolds with meaning. As Marcus Aurelius said, "The universe is change; our life is what our thoughts make it."

At its core, synchronicity is about trust. Trust that life is not chaotic and that when the world mirrors your inner world, it's worth paying attention. These moments – a timely call, a perfect turn, a resonating quote – are winks from the universe. When the inner and outer worlds harmonise, that's synchronicity. Not a command, but an invitation to follow the signs.

And maybe that's the lesson. Whether you call it intuition, fate, subconscious awareness or cosmic intelligence, the road knows things. Sometimes it speaks through hunches, chance meetings or strange timing. The trick is to listen – and to set your course with clarity.

Letting go of the map

Planning matters. But so does the ability to let it go. Overplanning or being rigid with your plan stifles discovery, whilst too little planning invites chaos. Virtually every day when you're on a longer tour, the road teaches you that a plan is a guideline, not a rule that must be obeyed. Even though I spent Chapter 2 explaining the importance of planning, too much structure on a motorcycle trip creates rigidity and stifles the very spirit that drew you to the road in the first place. Likewise, too much control in life keeps us rigid, stuck, closed and afraid to respond to what emerges. When you let go of the need to script every turn, you open yourself to the possibility of discovery.

That doesn't mean being reckless. It means riding with a plan in one hand and extending an open palm with the other (figuratively speaking). Some of the best rides I've ever done started with a rough idea and ended with something far better than I could have planned.

There's an old saying in philosophy and systems thinking: "The map is not the territory." Alfred Korzybski wrote that to remind us that no matter how detailed or accurate a map or mental model may be, it's still only a representation. It's not the real thing. A map will help you orientate yourself, but it's only a symbolic representation of the real thing that has been stripped of nuance, surprise and texture. In the same way, life is far richer than any plan can account for.

Werner Erhard took this further with a striking metaphor. He said that talking about transformation is no more than a representation, an image of the real thing. It's like eating the menu instead of the steak. I invite you to be here for the actual benefits of transformation, for the meal, not the menu. In other words, instead of experiencing life directly, most people live through interpretations shaped by their past experiences. They replay old stories in their head, apply outdated expectations, and miss the realities unfolding in front of them. Each moment is filtered through mental maps drawn from yesterday rather than encountered fresh. They react to the past and try to control the future, in the process, rarely meeting the present as it is.

It's like staring at a route planner while the best riding of your life is happening just outside your visor. You can't feel the road from a map. You can't taste the journey from a guidebook. At some point, you have to look up, lean in and ride. This is how life invites us to grow: not by forcing outcomes but by stepping into the unknown, responding to what you see in front of you, and recognising when grace has entered the moment.

The dead end that wasn't

When riding through the Adelaide Hills one time, I came across a narrow road with a sign saying, "No Through Road." Normally, I would have turned back. But something urged me on. The further I went, the more beautiful it became. The dense trees, the sunlight breaking through the mist, and a sense of complete peace made it stunning. At the supposed dead end, there was a small dirt path leading into a clearing where I found a retired rider fixing his old Norton. We ended up talking for two hours. He shared insights that struck me deeply, not just about bikes but also life. I left that day feeling lighter and with the sense that I was meant to have met him.

The road knows

Some riders believe the road teaches them. I agree. But not in a mystical, otherworldly sense. More in a grounded, rubber-on-tarmac, heart-in-your-throat way. The road humbles you. It surprises you. It reminds you who you are. It doesn't lie. And, sometimes, it speaks.

That voice might say, "Slow down here." Or "This is it." Or "Trust the turn."

Those who listen often find a deeper sense of fulfilment as well as greater safety. Being deeply aware of the moment means being present. It's not superstition. And when you ride with that level of awareness, the road stops being something to conquer. It becomes a thing you collaborate with.

Riding into the mystery

We live in a world that values certainty. But life requires us to embrace uncertainty and be comfortable with not being in control. Like riding, life is often messy. Sometimes we have to listen to something beyond logic, stepping into the mystery not to solve it but to experience it.

Joseph Campbell said, "Follow your bliss and doors will open where there were only walls." The invisible road is exactly that: a door that only appears once you commit to stepping forward. The rational mind wants guarantees. Intuition offers invitations.

Every time you gear up and head out, you have the chance to encounter something extraordinary, not just in the world around you but within yourself. The invisible road is always beneath your wheels, waiting, whispering, guiding. You don't need to see the entire road. You just need to trust the next curve, the next feeling, the next call from within. That's what it means to ride the invisible road, and to live guided by something deeper than certainty. You just have to be willing to listen.

Chapter 12

THE FINAL RIDE: ENDINGS, IDENTITY AND WHAT COMES AFTER

Ironically, it was a motorcyclist's death that changed the course of my life forever. On 3 June 1972, Dennis was killed when his Kawasaki Mach IV 750 hit a truck head on in suburban Sydney. He was just nineteen years old. He was bright, ambitious, and in his first year at Sydney University. He was the older brother of my school friend Robyne, and he was Ian's best mate.

What happened in the months that followed changed everything.

First, Robyne and I, once just friends, grew closer in our shared grief. She became my girlfriend and, eventually, my wife. We spent nineteen (mostly good) years together. Looking back, I doubt we would have ended up together if it weren't for Dennis's tragic accident.

Second, Ian became something of an adopted brother to me. We got to know each other through those raw months of loss. Over time, Ian became my closest friend.

At the time, I couldn't see the deeper significance of those changes. But they quietly set in motion relationships and life directions I could never have imagined. Ian was already riding bikes, and his girlfriend Sandra, who later became his wife, quickly bonded with Robyne. The four of us became close, sharing not only our friendship but also a growing passion for motorcycle touring. We spent countless weekends and holidays riding together, forging memories that would last a lifetime.

Looking back now, I see that Dennis's death was more than just a tragic

The Final Ride: Endings, Identity and What Comes After

event; it was a philosophical rupture, a turning point that rearranged lives and redirected futures and, in a tragic sort of way, gave birth to new beginnings. It was my first intimate brush with mortality since my father's untimely death when I was nine years old. That event was also a turning point that created lifelong shifts for our family. Both these incidents were fundamental in embedding within me a lifelong contemplation of the fragility of life and the importance of living fully while you can. In different ways, both of those heartbreaking moments led to the greatest transformations I've ever experienced.

Of the certainties in life, death is the one most feared and most certain – at least taxes can be minimised or avoided. From Ernest Becker's groundbreaking work in *The Denial of Death* to the existential insights of thinkers such as Viktor Frankl, Rollo May, and Martin Heidegger, the theme of mortality has been central to understanding human behaviour and growth. In their works, we find a common thread: that the awareness of death is not to be feared; rather, it can guide us towards deeper meaning and more authentic living.

In *Man's Search for Meaning*, Viktor Frankl suggests that it is precisely our awareness of death that gives life its meaning. Frankl observed that in the most harrowing circumstances, such as the concentration camps where he had been imprisoned, those who could find meaning in their suffering and face death with purpose were more likely to survive. Frankl's philosophy teaches us that death is not an end but a transition into a greater context. Similarly, the rider who understands the impermanence of life and faces the risks of the road with mindfulness and purpose can live more fully, in a constant state of engagement with the present moment.

This idea became more tangible to me as I grew older. Like most people, when I was younger, the idea of death was just an abstract concept, something far off on the horizon to which I never gave much thought. But in recent years, it has come closer, not in a morbid way, but in the quiet awareness that the body doesn't do what it used to. I have realised that courage in the face of death is essential for authentic living and a full life. It is only when we find the courage to confront our fear and anxiety about death that we find the courage to live more fully. I came to accept that death is a natural part of life – inevitable – and the certainty of it is out of our control. Just as a rider faces the challenges of the road, confronting our mortality allows us to steer our lives towards greater purpose. Gradually, I have come to understand what Marcus Aurelius meant when he said, "It's not death that we should fear, but we should fear never beginning to live."

Years after Dennis's death, I discovered Becker's *The Denial of Death*. That book also changed me. It gave voice to something I had long felt but could never fully articulate: that much of human behaviour – our striving, our clinging to find some sense of meaning in life – is largely shaped by our deep, often unconscious and, therefore, unspoken fear of death. Becker's insights offered me a framework for understanding not only the pain of those early losses but also the strange, beautiful ways that death continues to shape how we live.

Before he was a Pulitzer Prize–winning author, Becker was an academic misfit. A passionate, theatrical, fiercely independent thinker, he never did quite fit the mould of conventional academia. He was the kind of teacher who dressed up as King Lear to teach existential psychology, who used Shakespeare to dissect Freud, and who urged students to wrestle with mortality as a daily reality, not just as a philosophical abstraction.

His lectures weren't lectures in the conventional sense; they were more like theatrical performances. One day, he'd quote Kirkegaard on despair; the next, he'd act out Don Quixote's noble delusion to illuminate the human struggle for meaning. He blended anthropology, psychology, theology and literature into a defiant cocktail of insight and provocation. Students loved him. But many administrators didn't.

He was simply too "different" for some. Perhaps he was simply ahead of his time in some of his methods, using "info-tainment" in a conservative university environment. In just six years, Becker was let go from four universities, including a controversial dismissal from Simon Fraser University in Canada. While many students admired his passionate, theatrical and unconventional teaching style, he was too radical and independent-minded for the more traditional academic culture of the time. He once accused the modern university of "keeping people asleep" to the reality of death, while he, in every classroom, tried to wake them up to it. At SFU, his refusal to conform made him a target during a tense period of institutional change. It was 1969, a time of great cultural change. He didn't only challenge ideas; he also challenged the system itself. The real point I'm trying to make is that he thought and behaved differently from his generally conservative university colleagues of the time.

Like Becker, Scottish psychiatrist R.D. Laing refused to accept the orthodoxy of the time. He regularly challenged mainstream psychiatry, and, instead of seeing the patient as "broken", he suggested that society and families might be the ones who were sick. He once defined insanity thus: "Insanity, a perfectly rational adjustment to an insane world."

It is not hard to criticise "normal", as both Becker and Laing did regularly. Both regularly described "normal" as little more than being half-alive. It could be argued that being "normal" in modern society often means being alienated, asleep or less than fully alive. As a motorcyclist, I've often felt different and judged for my choice to ride. Riding forces you to see the world from another angle. I remember crossing the Hay Plains, wind buffeting me sideways, a storm brewing on one side, blistering sun on the other. In a car you'd hardly notice; but on a bike, you can't escape it. You lean in, stay awake, and face reality head on. Like Becker in the classroom and Laing with a patient, the road shakes you out of complacency and reminds you that life isn't meant to be lived half-asleep.

At the heart of Ernest Becker's work was a powerful idea: that human beings construct what he called "immortality projects" or "hero systems." These symbolic frameworks, such as beliefs, careers, religions, reputations, and roles, are designed to buffer us from the terror of death. They help us feel that our lives matter, that we in some way make aa difference and will endure beyond our physical end.

For the sake of clarity and simplicity, I'll call them *symbolic shells*. Becker's term was "immortality projects," but the image of a shell captures the same essence: something that both protects and confines. These shells give life structure and meaning, yet they can also harden into prisons if we cling to them too tightly.

Just as turtles, crabs, and lobsters carry shells to shield their soft bodies from harm, we carry symbolic shells to shield us from hurt, loss, and ultimately the fear of death. The danger is that we begin to identify with the shell and mistake it for the self. We start saying things like, "I am my job," or "I am my title," "I am a motorcyclist," forgetting that is but one small part of who we really are and that our true identity is far greater, deeper, and more mysterious than any single role.

Becker's point was that while the terror of death is universal, the form of the shell varies: one person's religion, another's career, another's ideology. What matters is recognising that these protective structures are not the essence of who we are, but temporary defences. Our challenge is to honour the role of these shells without confusing them for the whole of ourselves.

Symbolic Shells and the True Self

This diagram illustrates Ernest Becker's concept of immortality projects (hero systems), presented here as 'symbolic shells.' The concentric circles represent layers of identity: the outer symbolic shells, the middle layer of roles and identities, and at the centre, the True Self.

The Final Ride: Endings, Identity and What Comes After

Symbolic Shells and the True Self

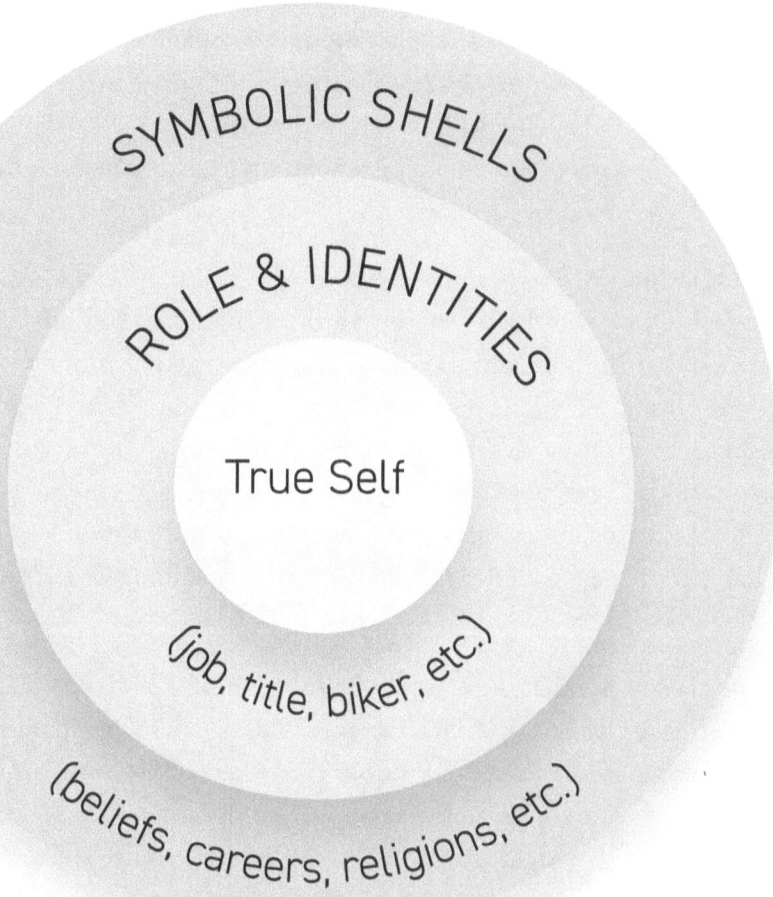

The danger lies in shrinking our identity and potential down to the size of a business card or a reputation. The symbolic shell creates a sense of safety, but it can also become a prison. A job, a relationship, a certain standing in society, a belief system; these are vital parts of being human, but none of them can capture the whole of who we are. They are simply a part of the mask that we present to the world – our curated, acceptable self. True fulfilment, Becker argued, comes when we loosen our grip on the shell and rediscover the raw aliveness underneath.

Becker knew this tension personally. His own career reflected both the promise and the cost of stepping outside prescribed roles. At Simon Fraser University in Vancouver, he challenged the safe orthodoxy of his colleagues and students. He refused to play by the unspoken rules of academia, and in doing so, he lost the security of a permanent post. After leaving SFU, he never again held a tenured position. Yet in this very act of defiance, he lived out his philosophy: that life is more than the masks we wear, and that sometimes the price of freedom is high.

Researching Becker reminded me of a rider I met on a long trip through outback Queensland. He was on an old BMW R100GS adventure bike. It seemed that both he and the bike were held together more with hope than good planning or organising. No GPS, a basic setup with no real plan. Just heading north to wherever the road ended. "I'm 74. I used to schedule every stop," he told me. "Now I just ride and see what shows up." He wasn't being reckless; he was just done living inside other people's expectations. That dusty, open-ended ride was his way of stepping outside the shell and riding his truth.

It's no surprise that the Pulitzer Prize–winning *The Denial of Death*, written while Becker was dying of cancer, reads more like a personal reckoning or spiritual manifesto than a textbook. He believed that most of what we do, our striving, our attachments, even our ambitions, are shaped by an unconscious effort to outwit death. We build lives not only to thrive but also to symbolically escape our terror of the reality of our mortality, and we attempt to do this through legacy, heroism, family, faith and accomplishment. We secretly seek immortality.

But instead of seeing fear of death as weakness, Becker saw in it the key to understanding ourselves and living more honestly, more humbly, and more courageously. It is a doorway, not a flaw. When we face it honestly, we can begin to live with more humility, clarity and courage.

I never met Becker, but I've felt his presence on the road. Motorcycling strips away illusions. It demands you face your fear and vulnerability. It doesn't let you pretend you're invincible. Every bend, every risk, every moment of stillness at the side of the road reminds you that this ride, indeed, this life, is fragile, fleeting and real. . It constantly reminds you that you're not.

In that spirit, here are four ways that Becker's insights ride in tandem with the deeper lessons of life on two wheels.

1. Every ride is a brush with mortality

On a bike, death is a constant possibility. You feel it in the crosswind pushing you off your line as you travel at 120 kph; in the corner where loose gravel crunches under your tyres; or in the wombat that lumbers onto the road just as you're exiting a blind turn. There's no barrier between you and the potential consequences.

Becker believed that the denial of death was the driving force behind much of human behaviour. We avoid the thought of our mortality by chasing control, status or comfort. But motorcycling makes such a denial impossible. You feel your vulnerability – and your aliveness – every moment you ride. And in a strange way, that feeling contributes to making it beautiful. The awareness doesn't shrink your life. It expands and sharpens it. You become more alert, more present, more grateful. You don't ride to tempt fate; you ride to acknowledge it. Fully. Consciously. With both hands on the bars. The motorcycle acknowledges mortality, even honours it.

2. Freedom through awareness, not escape

Modern culture sells freedom as escape: from work, from struggle and pain, from responsibility. *Buy our product, and you'll escape the mundanity of everyday life.* Becker argued that much of what we pursue in the name of freedom is essentially done to avoid acknowledging our mortality, or it is an attempt to escape a sense of meaninglessness or ignore the truth.

Motorcycling offers a freedom that lets you enter into life more fully.

You're not escaping life but, rather, releasing yourself from the illusion that everyday worries and duties are all there is to life. Riding demands your total attention – your mind, body, breath and awareness all locked into the present. I remember once cresting a ridgeline in the Snowy Mountains one crisp morning, the mist still clinging to the valleys below. No traffic, no noise, just the quiet hum of the engine and the wind threading through the trees. In that moment, I wasn't caught up in yesterday's regrets or tomorrow's plans. I wasn't performing a role or clinging to an identity that made demands on me. I was simply there, riding the road as it unfolded.

With nothing but the wind separating you from the world, motorcycling strips away illusions and distractions. You're not numbing or avoiding. You're alive to every curve, every gust, every choice. In this way, the bike becomes a truth-teller. Becker warns that we often hide in symbolic shells to feel secure, but riding the road doesn't let you hide. It invites you to shed those layers and meet life, raw and unscripted.

3. The road as Heroic Journey – but one that requires humility

Becker believed that we humans are driven by a need for heroism. We long to matter. To leave a mark. To be part of something bigger. But he warned that when our "hero projects" are built on ego or delusion, they become dangerous. The need to feel important outweighs the need to be real. When this happens, people are scapegoated and wars are waged.

As previously described, Joseph Campbell, who studied mythologies across cultures, framed the Hero's Journey as a timeless path: the call to adventure; the descent into challenge; the discovery of new truths; and the return, changed. But Campbell also reminded us that the true hero does not conquer the world and return with a trophy. Rather, they transcend their own limitations and come back bearing wisdom.

Motorcyclists know this journey firsthand. A long-distance ride can feel like an odyssey: an unknown horizon, trials of fatigue and weather, and moments of insight that arrive in silence. I once found myself broken down on a remote "C" road in Victoria. I was alone, the sun was sinking fast, and there was no phone reception. I was forced to sit in the stillness for about ninety minutes, with no distractions, no escape, just the humbling reality of vulnerability. That wasn't a failure. That was part of the initiation.

The road doesn't reward arrogance. It humbles you. It demands respect. Respect for terrain, for conditions, for your own limits. The real heroism of riding isn't loud. It's quiet, steady, aware. You learn to listen to the bike, to the wind, to your instincts. You learn that strength lies in adaptability, not dominance.

Becker didn't dismiss the Hero's Journey. He called for a mature version of it, one grounded in reality, mortality and service. And Campbell's map of the hero reminds us that the journey is never about proving how great you are. It's about discovering what truly matters and then returning with grace.

4. Legacy and meaning: What we leave behind

Becker's core idea was that we all try to transcend death symbolically. We all seek immortality. To be honoured and remembered. Whether through children, art, contribution or community, we strive to leave something behind that says, *I was here. I mattered. I made a difference.* (Perhaps this was one of the reasons I started to write this book – a tilt at immortality?)

Motorcycling may not seem like a legacy in the traditional sense, but it is. Every rider leaves echoes. Not just in the kilometres they've clocked, but in the people they rode with and the spirit they shared. Legacy isn't only what you leave behind. It's also what you awaken in others while you're still riding. Conversations at roadhouses. Stories swapped at twilight. Mateship forged under a shared sky.

I've known riders who are no longer with us, but their presence is still felt on every ride. In the memories, the laughter and the lessons they passed on. They didn't die. Their spirits ride on.

The road ends for all of us. But if we've ridden well, something will remain. Not monuments, but in moments. Not statues, but stories.

Final gear change

After researching Becker, it seems to me that the most alive people are those who face up to the terrifying truth of their existence and eventual demise, and still choose to live with passion, even in the face of death.

Motorcycling has taught me this.

You don't need to be fearless. You just need to be willing. Show up. Ride. Live not despite your limits but because of them.

Find meaning by leaning into that last curve, not by avoiding the end.

And perhaps, when the journey is done, be willing to leave behind not just rubber on the road but also something of yourself in the wind.

When the ride slows, the journey deepens

There's a moment near the end of every long ride where the landscape begins to feel familiar again. You start recognising signs and curves, even the light on the trees. The exhilaration of the unknown softens and is replaced by a quieter kind of joy: the knowledge that you've made it through, that the journey has changed you, and that home is close now.

This final chapter is written in that spirit.

It's not a goodbye. It's a reflection. A nod to the road I've travelled, and an opening to whatever comes next. Because while every ride eventually ends, the journey within – the ride down the open road inside each of us – has no finish line.

Knowing it doesn't last makes it matter more

Riding has always been a kind of homecoming for me. Whether I was

The Final Ride: Endings, Identity and What Comes After

rolling across dusty roads in the outback, carving down winding Victorian highlands, or just following a coastal breeze, being on the bike connected me to something larger, quieter and more honest than everyday life often allowed me.

Eventually, even the best roads run out of tarmac

Seven years ago, I was diagnosed with Parkinson's Disease. That's not something I ever expected to have to say, but it's real, and it's slowly reshaping what's possible for me physically. There's a creeping recognition that there will come a time, sooner than I'd like, when I'll have to stop riding. It's already influencing the type of bike I will get next. My last bike.

Parkinson's Disease is teaching me a new kind of life lesson that I never asked for. I am learning to receive that lesson with the same attitude I've always brought to the road: respect, presence, and a willingness to adapt. Yes, letting go of motorcycling is giving up a machine and a pastime, but it also involves my releasing a core part of my self-identity and how I've made sense of life up until now. The wind, the lean, the freedom, the solitude, the risk, the joy – all of it has been more than recreation. It's been revelation. Letting that go will be one of the most difficult things I've ever had to do.

But strangely, it's also opening something else in me.

When you can't ride the road, ride the meaning

I've always believed the road is a teacher. It shows you how to focus, how to trust, how to adapt. But it also teaches you how to let go. The best riders aren't just skilled at control, they're skilled at surrendering.

You can't control the weather, or a kangaroo bounding out of nowhere. Now, I'm learning that I can't control what my body is beginning to do. But I can control how I meet it.

That's the deeper teaching here. To ride well was much more than throttle control or balance. It was presence, attitude, awareness and acceptance.

These lessons still apply, even more so, when I'm off the bike.

In a strange way, I feel like I'm stepping into a new part of the same journey. Soon, I might not be able to ride through mountains anymore, but I'm learning to navigate terrain that's just as uncertain, just as demanding, and just as rich with meaning.

Beyond the shell: Letting go, letting be

At this stage of life, I find myself thinking about Ernest Becker's warning against living inside shells, the psychological constructs we create to shield ourselves from the discomfort of knowing that life is finite and that we're all going to die. The roles, achievements, reputations and routines that we have put so much energy into building and that we so strongly identify with become a kind of armour against the "ugly truth": our own mortality waits. But over time, that shell can become a prison.

Becker argued that most of us unconsciously build these shells to avoid facing our mortality. We strive to be important, remembered and admired – anything to keep the truth of impermanence at bay. But the price of that illusion is steep. We lose touch with the raw immediacy and natural joy of life. Instead, we live in symbols, not in experience. We eat the menu instead of enjoying the feast.

Motorcycling always offered me a way out of that trap. On the bike, there's no mask, no performance. Just the road, the wind, and the truth of the moment. It's hard to pretend when your whole body is listening, your attention sharpened, your life quite literally on the line. The ride cracks open the shell and invites you to feel what's real.

Now, Parkinson's is doing something similar. It's peeling away another layer of identity, my long-held role as a rider. And while that's painful, it's also liberating. It's a chance to let go not just of a bike but also the need to define myself by any one thing. To live not as "someone", but as something more open, more fluid.

Becker didn't see our fear of death as a flaw. He saw it as a gateway to living more honestly, humbly and courageously. And maybe that's my work now, to not cling to who I've been but, rather, meet what's coming with a quiet kind of dignity.

The bike may stop, but the ride won't be over. I'll just be shifting to a deeper gear.

Mortality isn't the end; it's the mirror

Becker wrote that our fear of death lies beneath much of what we do. We build, strive and distract ourselves in a grand effort to avoid the truth that everything ends. But real freedom, he argued, comes from facing death, not denying it.

Motorcycling prepared me for that truth more than I realised. Every ride held risk. Every corner demanded trust. Every journey was a reminder that life is fragile and, therefore, precious.

When I first started riding, death was a distant shadow. Now, it rides pillion. Oddly enough, I don't find that frightening. Knowing the road ahead is finite makes the present more vivid. That's what Becker pointed to: awareness of death makes life meaningful. Not morbid, but deeply meaningful. It urges you to ride while you can. To love while you can. To speak truth. To stop pretending there will always be more time.

What comes after the last ride?

So, what happens when I can't ride anymore?

I'll grieve, no doubt. I'll miss the long open roads, the hum of tyres over bitumen, the quiet bond between rider and machine. I'll miss riding with Ian. I'll miss the version of myself that only the bike could reveal.

But I will not stop being a motorcyclist.

Because being a rider isn't just something I do. It's part of who I've become. The qualities that riding cultivated, things like resilience, courage, presence, adaptability and wonder – they won't disappear when the engine stops. They'll stay with me. They'll guide how I face what's next.

Maybe I'll write more. Maybe I'll teach. Maybe I'll sit under a gum tree and simply be. Whatever comes, I won't resist it. I'll meet it with curiosity, as if it were another unplanned detour, just like those I took on some of the best days on tour.

Endings aren't endings; they're thresholds

This book began with the joy of motorcycling. It ends with something even more enduring. Because riding doesn't just teach you how to live well. It teaches you how to face endings with grace. Not in a dramatic, heroic way but in a way that is deeply human. Fully aware. Grateful. Present.

To ride well is to live well. And to live well is to reach the end without regret. To say, *I rode as far as I could, as deeply as I could, and I didn't hold back.*

So now, as I look beyond the saddle, I don't see a void. I see another kind of beginning. I don't know what's next, but whatever it is, I'll meet it with the same spirit I brought to every ride:

Helmet off. Heart open. Eyes forward.

The road doesn't really end. It just changes form. Even after the final corner, there's still a journey unfolding: within you, between you and others, and perhaps beyond this life. I don't claim to know what lies ahead. But I trust that the spirit of riding has prepared me well.

One Last Ride

If you've ridden this far with me through the journey of this book, through these stories and reflections, thank you. I hope they stirred something in you: a question, a memory, a sense of recognition. Because whatever path you walk or ride, there will come a time when something ends. A loss. A change you didn't choose.

When that moment comes, may you remember this:

The end of the ride is not the end of the rider.

And maybe, just maybe, what comes next is the most meaningful road of all.

The Road Within Never Ends

The outer journey may reach its final curve. But the Open Road Within continues, through memory, legacy, and the impact we leave behind.

So, this isn't just the end of a chapter. It's a bow to what has been, and a nod to what still might come. To you, the reader, may your road be long, surprising and meaningful. May you take the curves with grace, the detours with humour and the unknowns with trust. And when the day comes to let go – of a ride, a dream or a way of life – may you remember:

The bike may stop. But the rider within rides on.

EPILOGUE - THE ROAD STILL CALLS

When I first had the idea to write a book that combined two things I know well – motorcycling and personal development - the reason I did it was to leave something for my three children to remember me by. And, hopefully, they'd understand more about me and my passion for motorcycles.

Somehow, it took up a life of its own.

I never set out to write a book that *taught* anything. I set out to *share* what the road has taught me. Over 800,000 kilometres and five decades, I've learned that motorcycling isn't an escape. It's an entry. An entry into presence, courage, flow and meaning. Into you – or, more precisely, learning about you.

Some people finish reading a book with a sense of finality. I hope you close this one with the urge to open a map. Or better still, to walk out to the garage, dust off the bike, and fire it up.

Because the road never truly ends.

It twists and turns, disappears into fog, reappears over a ridge, and sometimes, when you're brave enough to trust it, it reveals something extraordinary not just about the world but also yourself.

This book has been my way of parking the bike for a moment, taking off the helmet, and sitting down across from you. Dusty, exhilarated, humbled and grateful to pass on a few stories and scars, hard-won lessons and quiet revelations. Not as an expert, but as a fellow traveller. A rider. A human trying to make sense of it all.

If there's one thing I'd urge you to carry with you, it's this: life, like the road, rarely unfolds as planned. But if you lean in – into the curve, into the wind, into uncertainty – you'll find your rhythm. You'll discover that the very things you feared might break you were actually shaping you.

So, whether you're straddling a motorcycle, standing at a crossroads, or staring down the next chapter of your life… listen. The road is calling.

Take it.

www.ingramcontent.com/pod-product-compliance
Lightning Source LLC
Chambersburg PA
CBHW060354080526
44583CB00012B/301